WHICH IS C

We had drank a quart of lemonade.
We had drunk a quart of lemonade.

Hal was hungry, he had worked a long day.
Hal was hungry; he had worked a long day.

There are three desk's in the room.
There are three desks in the room.

He asked me to lie my shirt on the ironing board.
He asked me to lay my shirt on the ironing board.

There are less people at the conference than there
were last year.
There are fewer people at the conference than there
were last year.

Lack of sleep can effect work performance.
Lack of sleep can affect work performance.

Don't act like you're surprised.
Don't act as if you're surprised.

If you're unsure of any of these, you're not alone.
Grammar 101 can help.

(The second sentence in each pair is correct.)

Also available in this series

WRITING 101
SPELLING 101

GRAMMAR
101

CLAUDIA SORSBY

Produced by The Philip Lief Group, Inc.

St. Martin's Paperbacks

Produced by The Philip Lief Group, Inc.

GRAMMAR 101

Copyright © 1996 by The Philip Lief Group, Inc.

ISBN: 0-312-95973-7

Printed in the United States of America

St. Martin's Paperbacks edition/August 1996

10 9 8 7 6 5 4 3

Contents

CONTENTS

CONTENTS

Introduction

Many people are intimidated by grammar, but they shouldn't be. It seems threatening, with lots of scary technical terms that don't make a whole lot of sense, and lots of even scarier rules that don't seem to serve any purpose.

Important thing to remember about grammar is this: *You already know it.* You use grammar every day, all of the time, with every thought you think and every sentence you utter. You're using it to read this book. Any four-year-old child who has learned to speak understands grammar better than any computer (to the undying envy of artificial intelligence scientists). The trick is to combine the understanding you developed unconsciously as a child with knowledge of the formal terms and rules you need now.

Grammar is nothing more than a system for assigning names and terminology to things and functions that everyone already understands, so that we can communicate intelligently.

If a teacher grades your paper and says, "Well, you received a low grade because I couldn't understand your sentences," that's not very helpful. You won't know what you did wrong, so you won't be able to fix it in the future. But if the teacher says, "I gave you a low grade because you were inconsistent with your subject-verb agreement," that tells you something concrete. All you need to do is search through this book, refresh your understanding of subject-verb agreement, and your grammar will improve.

Most people associate grammar with endless, dull English classes. Once those classes are over, who needs it? But once you're out of school, grammar matters even more. Your boss isn't going to take the time to critique your memos for you; he or she will just read what you write and decide whether you know your stuff on the basis of your copy. If it's unclear or full of mistakes, you are in much more trouble than your grammar teacher ever gave you.

Part of why grammar matters is that spoken language is often quite different from written language. We all say things we would never write, such as "I gotta get outta here," instead of "I have to get out of here." In the 1990's, that's as it should be. When you are speaking with someone, you give all sorts of physical cues that help make your meaning clear; you change your tone, you alter your facial expression, you make gestures. But when you're writing, you can't do any of those things. Your reader has to rely on your written words alone to understand your meaning. Since you can't pause, you need to use the right punctuation. Again, people tend to know this without necessarily realizing it, and intuitively write more formally than they speak.

This book offers you 101 rules that will help you to better understand standard English grammar. You will learn the names of the parts of speech, and the rules that govern how they are used. You will also find the rules of syntax that determine how sentences should be put together, and those that determine the punctuation and capitalization of sentences. If you're in school, you can use this book to help you write better in all of your classes, not just to get better grades on grammar tests. If you're out of school, this book can serve as a handy reference tool, no matter your profession or hobby interests.

To make your life a bit easier, many of the examples and exercises in this book follow the story of the fictional Mr. Ooze, a primordial man who will be acquiring language as the book progresses. Be patient with him, because he won't be acquiring language the normal way children do, all at once; he'll be learning in the order of the book's rules and definitions.

If you would like more information on specific problems in writing, there are two other books in this series that may be of use to you: *Writing 101*, which offers instruction on the finer points of writing; and *Spelling 101*, which provides basic instruction on how to spell and pronounce one of the most notoriously pesky languages on the planet.

I strongly recommend that you invest in a good dictionary, such as *The Merriam-Webster Dictionary*. A good thesaurus, such as *Roget's 21st Century Thesaurus,* edited by Barbara Kipfer, is also helpful. On CD-ROM, the *American Heritage Dictionary* provides the power of a dictionary cross-referenced with hyperlinking to a thesaurus. For guidelines on specifics for book publishing, *The Chicago Manual of Style* remains the standard.

I could not have written this book without the help of Sahngmie Lah, who did much of the preliminary work. Gary M. Krebs, my editor in New York, put up with the vicissitudes of transatlantic mail while I was living and working in England. And of course, none of this would have gotten done without the constant encouragement of my husband, Daniel Hillman. Any errors are, of course, mine alone.

—CHCQS
October 1995
Cambridge, England

The Rules

1. Remember That Parts of Speech Can Change, Depending on Usage

To make talking about language easier, all words are assigned categories, which are known as parts of speech. There are thousands of words in the English language; by breaking them down into groups, it becomes much simpler to understand how they work. Then you can see clearly how words fit together to make sentences. All told, there are eight main parts of speech, which will be discussed in the next several rules.

The important thing to remember is that the same word can fit into different categories at different times, depending on how it is being used in a given sentence.

EXAMPLE: Do you have a *saw*?

EXAMPLE: We *saw* my teacher at the heavy metal concert last night.

In the first example, the word *saw* refers to a particular thing, a type of tool used to cut wood (see Rule 2). In the second, the word *saw* refers to the action of having seen a person at a particular place and time in the past (see Rule 5).

Don't be confused. Much of the playfulness of the English language comes directly from this little feature, the possibility of double meaning or misunderstanding. Be patient with yourself as you recognize the parts of speech and how a word can take on new meanings depending on its context in a sentence.

3

2. Know That Nouns, Such as *Tree* or *Chicago*, Are People, Places, Things, or Ideas

Anything that can enact or receive action is a noun. Nouns name things, such as people, places, objects, or ideas.

EXAMPLES: girl, boy, town, river, book, demon, computer, spider, boredom, liberty.

Compound nouns are nouns made up of more than one word.

EXAMPLES: litter box, false teeth, concert hall, human sacrifice.

Most of the trouble with nouns arises from one of two areas. First is the question of plural forms. In most cases, you simply add the letter *s*.

EXAMPLES: weasel   weasels
             idiot   idiots
             jewel   jewels
             theft   thefts

However, there are many exceptions to this rule, and they cause problems. For example, many nouns that don't take -*s* to become plural take -*es*. If you are ever unsure of what the right plural form for a noun is, don't hesitate to look it up. Types of animals can be especially tricky; native speakers of English rarely realize just how many irregularities they use every day.

EXAMPLES: dog   →   dogs

BUT: mouse   →   mice
           ox   →   oxen
           deer   →   deer

Collective nouns refer to groups. *Family* is a good example of a collective noun. It refers to a group of people, who are related to each other, and make up a specific group, different from other groups. Unfortunately, many collective nouns are completely irregular, and so you have to memorize them.

Irregular collective nouns can take either a singular verb form or a plural verb form, depending on the intended meaning of your sentence. The verb will usually be singular if you are considering individual members of the collective noun group.

EXAMPLES: The majority of college students *are* under age twenty-two.
The Senate majority *is* debating the smoking issue.

The team *wins* every year.
The team *are* the best nine players in the country.

The army *recruits* members from our campus every spring

Keep in mind that collective nouns like *news*, *physics*, and *orchestra* always take the singular verb form.

EXAMPLES: The news *is* so depressing sometimes.
Physics *is* something I will never grasp.
The orchestra *plays* this piece beautifully.

Also be aware that collective nouns like *media* and *phenomena* always take the plural verb form.

EXAMPLES: The media *are* hounding that poor football star again.

Those phenomena *tend* to upset the general public.

EXERCISE

Mr. Ooze has just discovered nouns, and he is beginning to describe his world. Of course, he will make some errors as he tries to create plural forms and use collective nouns. Correct his mistakes in the sample of his first words below.

Mr. Ooze walked along, muttering to himself as he thought about things:
"Land . . . skys . . . trees . . . water . . . rockes . . . foxs . . . familys . . . cave . . . fire . . . stars . . . lawyers . . . bushs . . . birdes . . . dirt . . . teames . . . paths . . . streams . . . pondes . . . frogs . . . lilys . . . mosquitos . . . bugs . . . daisyes . . . roses . . . clouds."

3. Know the Two Kinds of Nouns: Common (as in *Tree*) and Proper (as in *Chicago*)

Overall, there are two kinds of nouns: common nouns and proper nouns. Common nouns refer to general people, places, or things, while proper nouns name specific ones. You designate a noun as a proper noun by capitalizing it.

COMMON NOUNS: woman, country, monument

PROPER NOUNS: Clint Eastwood, England, the Leaning Tower of Pisa

Sometimes a writer will personify an abstract idea; in such cases, it should also be capitalized.

EXAMPLE: Although *Death* was on holiday, he was as bored as any other tourist wearing a Hawaiian shirt.

Notice, here, that *Hawaiian* is also capitalized, since it refers to a specific state.

EXERCISE:

Look around you, and for five minutes write down every noun that you see. Be sure to capitalize all proper nouns, including the "M" and "O" in *Mr. Ooze*.

4. Know That Pronouns, Such as *I*, *It*, and *She*, Take the Place of Nouns

A pronoun is nothing more than a word that stands in for another word in a sentence. The original word is called the pronoun's antecedent. Pronouns are handy, because it would be annoying to have to keep repeating the same name over and over. Pronouns solve this problem.

ANNOYING: Mr. Ooze sat by the lake. Mr. Ooze was hungry, but Mr. Ooze was tired of getting Mr. Ooze's food from the bushes nearby.

BETTER: Mr. Ooze sat by the lake. *He* was hungry, but *he* was tired of getting *his* food from the bushes nearby.

All the italicized words in the second paragraph are pronouns, referring to Mr. Ooze.

There are seven kinds of pronouns altogether. That sounds like a lot, but you use them all of the time, and you probably don't even think twice about them. (Most of them will be discussed in Rules 11 through 16; one kind, relative pronouns, will be discussed later, in Rule 38.)

5. Know That Verbs, Such as *Go* or *Act*, Express Actions or Conditions

Verbs are as much a part of language as nouns. More, in fact. While every single thing is a noun, everything that you do is a verb. If you are just sitting around, breathing, you are performing two actions: sitting and breathing. Both of those are expressed by verbs.

Most verbs are described as "action" words, because they indicate something is occurring. When you are doing things, you can: walk, talk, think, hop, tackle, knit, type, write, sing, play, or any of thousands of other things. Some verbs are called linking verbs, because they express condition; they show you how or what things are. Linking verbs include the verbs *to be*, *to seem*, and *to appear*. To put it plainly, a verb either *does* something (action) or *is* something (linking).

Verbs take subjects, which show who or what is performing the action of the verb. The subjects are generally either nouns or pronouns. Together, verbs and nouns are the building blocks of language.

EXAMPLE: Mr. Ooze runs.

In the above example, the verb is *to run*, and Mr. Ooze is the subject of the verb, since he is the one doing the running.

9

EXERCISE

Take five minutes and think of all the things you like to do most. Write down all of the verbs involved.

6. Know the Three Points of View: First-Person (*I*), Second-Person (*You*), and Third-Person (*His/Her/It*)

This is not a fancy way of saying that you should know yourself. English has three points of view, which are known as first-, second-, and third-person. They can be either singular or plural, which refers to their number.

In the sentence "I am alone in a room," the subject is *I*. Any time a writer or speaker tells a story through *I*, that is known as first person. Since the *I* only refers to one person, it's called first person singular. In the sentence "We ate the popcorn," however, the subject *we* refers to the speaker and other individuals; that is known as first person plural.

If the writer wants to address a specific person, as in the sentence "You will eat the popcorn," the subject is *you*. This is known as second person. If the writer wants to address a group of twenty people, the subject is still *you* and the sentence remains the same: "You will eat the popcorn." In other words, there is no such thing as second person plural. Although some people use *y'all* or *you all* in speech, the expression is nonstandard because "all of" is implied in *you*.

Third person refers to *him* or *her* — not the individual who is speaking or being addressed, but rather, the one who is the subject of conversation. If the writer is referring to an object, then the sexless *it* should be used. If several people are being discussed,

11

the speaker would refer to *them*, which is known as third person plural. In the English language, plurals don't assign sex; *they* and *them* can refer to mixed groups of men and women, or separate groups of men or women.

7. Know the Three Cases: *Subjective, Objective,* and *Possessive*

The grammatical term *case* is a perfect example of something that sounds much more complicated than it really is. In English, *case* refers to a category that names the functions of nouns and pronouns in a given sentence. When you decide what case a word is in, you are figuring out what that word is doing in that sentence.

The next thing to realize is that there are only three cases. There are more grammatical roles a noun or pronoun can play, of course, but in terms of endings and spellings changing, you only have to worry about three. These three cases are called the subjective, objective, and possessive.

The subjective, or nominative case, as it is often known, is used to refer to the subject of a sentence, the person or thing performing the action (see Rule 17).

EXAMPLE: *Mr. Ooze* sat by the river. After a while, a *bear* came along.

In the example above, Mr. Ooze is the subject of the first sentence, because he is the one who is performing the action of sitting. In the second sentence, the bear is the subject, because he is the one who came along.

The objective case is used to refer to the person or thing to whom the action is done.

EXAMPLE: Mr. Ooze looked at *him*.

In the example above, *him* is the object of the sentence, because *him* refers to the bear Mr. Ooze looked at.

The possessive case is used to show the idea of ownership, or possession.

EXAMPLE: The bear asked, "Would you like some of *my* berries?"

In the example above, *my* is a possessive pronoun (see Rule 51 for more on these). It is in the possessive case, to show that the berries belong to the talking bear.

There is another case that exists, but there are no spelling changes for it. A verb can take a direct object, as you have seen, but it can also take what is known as an indirect object. Indirect object pronouns are the same as direct object pronouns.

EXAMPLES: I gave the book to *Bob*.
I gave the book to *him*.
He gave *me* a letter in return.

In the first sentence, *the book* is the direct object of the verb to give, since it is the thing I gave. *Bob* is the indirect object, since I gave the book to him. In the second sentence, *him* is the indirect object pronoun, referring to that lucky guy Bob. In the third sentence, the pronoun *me* is the indirect object, while the letter is the direct object that is being given.

Since pronouns generally change their spelling as they change case, it is important to understand what case you need in any given sentence. If you find yourself confused, just go back to the basics and ask yourself, "Now, what is this word doing in this sentence?" Then you will know which case to use. (For more on pronouns, see Rule 11.)

8. Understand the Importance of Word Order

In English, word order matters. The classic example is the difference between the two phrases "dog bites man" and "man bites dog." These mean completely different things, and yet the only difference between them is the order of the words. To write well, you must understand the importance of word order.

The most basic structure for an English sentence is subject/verb/object. Thus, in the first example above, the dog is the subject of the sentence; he is performing the action of biting, and the man is the object, receiving the action of the bite. In the second example, the subject and object are reversed, and the dog is bitten by the man.

That said, there are an infinite variety of ways in which that basic structure can be changed. Language would be unspeakably dull if all of our sentences were forced to follow that same rigid pattern; luckily, we have a lot more freedom than that. For example, the passive voice and the imperative (see Rules 52 and 53, respectively) tend to change the order of words around. We also have a technique, called inversion, which we commonly use to signal that a question is being asked.

STANDARD ORDER: That's what you think.

INVERSION: Is that what you think?

15

Vary your word order to add interest to your writing, but remember that clarity is your ultimate goal. Sometimes simple sentences are best, while on other occasions something a little more jazzy is called for. It's up to you to decide.

9. Be Sure That All Parts of Your Sentences (Nouns, Verbs, Pronouns, Adjectives, etc.) Agree Properly

As with many other things, English requires agreement; that is, forms should match, or agree. This is one of the guiding principles of the language, but it's also the source of many careless errors.

Agreement applies to almost all parts of speech. It is terribly important, because without it, language becomes overwhelmingly confusing. For example, if I say that "I likes Ike," the verb is not agreeing with the subject. This is confusing, because you, the reader, have no way of knowing what I really meant to say. Did I mean that someone else likes Ike, and I used the wrong pronoun? Or, did I mean that I like Ike, and I used the wrong form of the verb? In many cases, you could probably figure out what I meant from context, but not always. If I say something about my new "male cow," you would again be confused, since by definition cows are female. Do I mean that I have acquired a bull, or a cow? By using an adjective (see Rule 22) that cannot possibly agree with the noun it is describing, I have again confused you, the reader.

In the following pages, the concept of agreement will be mentioned frequently. Do not underestimate its importance, because it underlies most of our language.

10. Make Sure Pronouns, Such as *He* and *They*, Agree with the Words to Which They Refer

Pronouns have already been defined as words that stand in for other words (see Rule 4). To make it clear what word a given pronoun replaces, the pronoun must agree in person, number, and gender.

This is quite simple to do in practice, and you do it all of the time, unconsciously. If, for example, you are writing something about Mr. Ooze in the third person, your pronouns referring to Mr. Ooze should stay in the third person. Since there is only one Mr. Ooze, he is singular, so you should consistently use singular pronouns, not plural. Since Mr. Ooze is a man, you should use masculine pronouns, not feminine or neuter.

Of course, nothing is easy all of the time. It can be difficult to determine the correct forms to use with both indefinite and relative pronouns, for example (see Rules 12 and 36, respectively). Most commonly, however, problems crop up when sentences get complicated. If the pronoun is far away from its antecedent, a writer may lose track. The only way to deal with this is to be aware of the potential problem and check your work several times. Most of writing is rewriting, and this is one of the reasons why.

11: Recognize Personal Pronouns, Such as *You*, *Him*, *Our*, and *Their*

Personal pronouns refer to people or things. They have three different forms, depending on what case they are in (if you've forgotten what that means, don't panic; see Rule 7). These are some of the most common words in the language; you use them all the time.

First Person

Case	Singular	Plural
Nominative/Subjective	I	we
Possessive	my, mine	our, ours
Objective	me	us

Second Person

Case	Singular	Plural
Nominative/Subjective	you	you
Possessive	your, yours	your, yours
Objective	you	you

Third Person

Case	Singular	Plural
Nominative/Subjective	he, she, it	they
Possessive	his, her, hers, its	their, theirs
Objective	him, her, it	them

You use personal pronouns to avoid having to repeat the name of the person or people you are talking about again and again. They're also helpful in showing possession, as in the statement, "Let go of *my* purse!"

Notice that the third person singular includes a masculine set of pronouns (he, him, his), a feminine set (she, her, hers), and a neuter set (it, its).

EXERCISE

Help Mr. Ooze get used to the idea that he can use personal pronouns, rather than repeating himself. Rewrite the following sentences, inserting the correct pronouns.

Mr. Ooze see tadpole.
Mr. Ooze bite tadpole.
Tadpole brother chases Mr. Ooze.
Mr. Ooze run.

12. Recognize Indefinite Pronouns, Such as *Anybody, Most, Either,* and *Each*

Indefinite pronouns are used when you need to refer to someone or something whose identity or number is not known. In the preceding sentence, both *someone* and *something* are indefinite pronouns themselves. A list of the indefinite pronouns follows:

all	everyone	nothing
another	everything	one
anybody	few	other
anyone	most	some
anything	neither	somebody
both	nobody	someone
each	none	something
either	no one	

The tricky thing about indefinite pronouns is keeping track of their agreement. The main problem arises when trying to decide whether or not to use singular or plural forms. For example, in the sentence "*most* of the eggs *are* rotten," the verb is plural, since most is clearly referring to a group of eggs. However, in the sentence "*most* of the soufflé *is* burnt," *most* is referring to one part of something, the poor soufflé, and so it requires a singular verb.

The indefinite pronoun *one* has some specific uses. It is used as an impersonal form, either to show universality or to avoid being limited to either the masculine or the feminine. It can sound rather formal, however.

EXAMPLE: Moving to a new place is always hard, but it's worst when *one* is alone. *One* often feels lost in a new town.

Since the above sentences do not name any specific person, they require indefinite pronouns. Using the second person (*you*) is usually considered too informal, and it also changes the meaning of the sentence: The point is that anyone can feel lost in a new town, not just you, the reader. In common speech, people will often use the pronoun *you* in this situation, since they can make it clear through their gestures that they mean a universal *you*. However, when writing, those extra cues aren't available, so writers have to be a bit more careful.

13. Recognize Interrogative Pronouns, Such as *Who* and *When*

Interrogative pronouns are used to ask questions. The most common are: *what*, *which*, and *who*.

When you ask a question with the pronoun *what*, you are generally trying to find information about a specific thing or event.

EXAMPLES: *What* happened?
What did you do?
What did she say?

In each of the above examples, the pronoun *what* stands in for an event. Something happened, you did something, she said something, and the questioner wants to know about it.

Which is used in situations where there are several possible outcomes, and you are trying to find out *which* one among them occurred.

EXAMPLES: There were six kittens in the litter. *Which* one had brown spots?
The road forks here: *Which* way did that darn cat go?

In both of these questions, there are at least two possible answers. In the first, we know that there were six kittens, and that only one of them had brown spots. The second states that there are two possible routes to follow, and the questioner wants to know whether the cat turned left or right.

Who asks for a specific identity—the name of an actual person.

EXAMPLE: *Who* keeps moving my chair?
To *whom* did you give the microfilm?
Who are you?

In the first example, someone keeps moving the chair, and the speaker is trying to identify that person. In the second sentence, *who* appears in the objective case form, *whom*. The question here is not who performed the action (as in the previous example), but rather who received it. If you wanted to rephrase that sentence using the possessive form, you could write "*Whose* microfilm is that?" In the third example, the nominative/subjective form *who* is used because *who* is the subject of the sentence.

Notice that if the answer is not a person, then the question should be rephrased. For example, if a supernatural force keeps moving my chair, I might answer, "The question isn't *who* keeps moving my chair, but *what*; it's a poltergeist!" A questioner who is unsure might ask, "Who, or what, keeps moving your chair?"

Demonstrative pronouns do just that; they point out, or demonstrate, things or people. They also draw attention to the relationship between the things being pointed out and the speaker. They can also be used as adjectives (see Rule 22), in which case they are known as demonstrative adjectives.

The best thing about demonstrative pronouns is that there are only four of them.

Singular	Plural
this	these
that	those

This and *these* are used to indicate immediacy or closeness, while *that* and *those* are used to indicate distance. This closeness or distance is defined as relative to the speaker.

EXAMPLES: Mr. Ooze wants *this* rock, not *that* one.
Mr. Ooze wants *these* rocks, not *those*.

In the first sentence, *this* and *that* are being used to demonstrate the difference between two rocks, the one that Mr. Ooze wants and the one he does not want. Notice that the pronoun tells you that the rock he wants is closer than the one he doesn't. If he wanted the rock that was farther away, he would want *that* rock (the one that is far), not *this* one (the one that is near). The same logic applies to the second sentence; the only difference is that it refers to

25

two groups of rocks, and therefore uses the plural forms.

EXERCISE:

Fill in the correct demonstrative pronouns in the following sentences.

I want this donut, not _____ donuts.
_____ child is well-behaved, but those children are minions of the Dark One.
_____ are not the ugliest pants in the store, those are.
I like _____ painting here, but not _____ one there.

15. Recognize the Reciprocal Pronouns: *Each Other* and *One Another*

Reciprocal pronouns are handy little words that help you separate the actions of multiple actors, or subjects. There are two pairs of them: *each other* and *one another*.

EXAMPLES: The twins looked at *each other* and grinned.
They often helped *one another* with their homework.

In the first sentence, there are two people, and each one is doing the same thing. The reciprocal pronoun *each other* makes it clear that each twin is looking at the other, rather than both twins looking together out at someone else. In the second sentence, *one another* serves the same function, by specifying who the twins helped.

EXERCISE

Rewrite the following paragraph, putting in reciprocal pronouns wherever they would be appropriate.

Mr. Ooze looked at the cat. The cat looked at Mr. Ooze. He wanted a cat as a pet, and he liked big marmalade cats like this one. He hoped that this cat would stay with him. He thought he could take care of the cat, and the cat could take care of him. Out loud he said, "I wonder what his name is," and was quite surprised when the cat answered, "Wesley."

16. Recognize Reflexive Pronouns, Such as *Itself* and *Yourselves*

To say that something is reflexive means that it refers back to itself. Reflexive pronouns do just that; they are personal pronouns with *-self* or *-selves* tacked on.

Person	Number	Reflexive pronouns
First	Singular	myself
Second	Singular	yourself
Third	Singular	himself
		herself
		itself
		oneself
First	Plural	ourselves
Second	Plural	yourselves
Third	Plural	themselves

Some verbs demand reflexive pronouns. If Mr. Ooze does something to amuse Mr. Ooze, he needs a reflexive pronoun to express that: "Mr. Ooze amused *himself*."

Sometimes reflexive pronouns are used for emphasis.

EXAMPLE: After having been sick and weak for so long, it was a big day when Mr. Ooze was able to dress *himself* again.

In the example above, *himself* is being used to emphasize the fact that when he was ill, Mr. Ooze was unable to dress himself, and now that he's better, he can do it again. When reflexive pronouns are used for emphasis this way, they are known as intensive pronouns. Intensive pronouns are the same as reflexive pronouns, except that their purpose is exclusively to emphasize the nouns to which they refer.

17. Know That a Complete Sentence Must Include a Subject and a Verb

A sentence is a group of words representing a fully realized thought; a complete sentence must include a subject and a verb. In other words, at its most basic level, a sentence must express what is happening (verb), and who is doing it (subject).

Of course, most sentences can and do include other words, which will be discussed. When discussing sentences, grammarians generally divide them into two pieces: the subject and the predicate. The predicate is everything in the sentence other than the subject.

EXAMPLE: Mr. Ooze *walked far into the woods, whistling cheerfully.*

In the above example, Mr. Ooze is the subject of the sentence, and everything that follows his name makes up the predicate. The predicate expresses what is going on in the sentence.

In sentences with linking verbs such as *to be*, the parts of the predicate that describe the subject are called the predicate nominative. They can also be called the subject complement.

EXAMPLE: The dog is *wet and angry*.

In this case, the whole underlined part of the sentence is the predicate; and *wet and angry* make up the predicate nominative (or subject complement), since they describe the soggy dog.

31

Sometimes the subject can be understood, meaning that you don't actually have to write it out. If the house is on fire and your sister yells "Run!" you understand, even though she has only yelled out a verb. It is understood that you are the subject of the sentence, since you're the one who's going to be doing the running (see Rule 53 on the imperative).

EXERCISE

Underline the subjects in the following sentences (or write them in if they are omitted).

Mr. Ooze went to the shopping mall.
The security guard saw him try to eat a CD.
Stop!
Startled, Mr. Ooze ran into the bookstore.

18. Be Sure That Subjects and Verbs Are Always in Agreement, Such as *The Leaves Change* and *The Court Finds*

One of the most common mistakes among writers is that they forget that verbs must agree with their subjects, in both number and person. The good news is that this is usually easy to fix (see Rules 19 and 20).

Person	Singular	Plural
First	I like Mr. Ooze.	We like Mr. Ooze.
Second	You like Mr. Ooze.	
Third	He or she likes Mr. Ooze.	They like Mr. Ooze.

For regular verbs, this is pretty straightforward. Irregular verbs can cause trouble, but they are manageable because there aren't that many of them. Moreover, most of the irregular verbs are used quite frequently, so writers tend to learn them simply through daily use.

The real trouble arises when the sentences become complicated. The subject might not appear right before the verb, but get moved further away in the sentence. Once the subject and verb are separated, it's easy to miss a lack of agreement. Be especially careful in these cases.

EXERCISE

Fix any subject-verb problems in the following sentences.

Mr. Ooze love big cats.
Wesley, the big cat, love mice.
The mouse doesn't love Wesley.
The mouse love cheese.
All of the mice loves cheese.
Mr. Ooze and Wesley also loves cheese.
They all loves cheese.

19. Know the Difference Between Transitive Verbs (Such as *To Set the Table*) and Intransitive Verbs (Such as *To Exist*)

One of the main distinctions between verbs is whether or not they are transitive or intransitive. Once again, grammarians have taken simple ideas and given them scary terms, for no discernible reason. A transitive verb is simply one that does its action to something, and thus takes an object. An intransitive verb does not need an object.

TRANSITIVE VERB: I *shot* the television.

INTRANSITIVE VERB: I *breathed*.

In the first example, the unlucky television receives the actio, of my shooting. In the second example, the only thing occurring is my breathing. No object is required.

Some verbs can be either transitive or intransitive, depending on how they are used in a given sentence. For example, the verb *to play* can be used transitively, as in the sentence "We all *played* tag." Here, the game of tag is the object, since it is what we played. However, the same verb can be used intransitively, as in the sentence "Yesterday afternoon we *played*."

Linking verbs, such as *to be*, *to seem*, or *to become*, are generally intransitive. However, they often need something (other than the object of a verb) to complete their meaning. In the sentence, "He seemed *embarrassed*," the word *embarrassed* is not an object. It describes the subject of the sentence, and so it is called a subject complement (see Rules 17 and 87).

20. Know the Different Parts of Verbs (*Stems, Infinitives, Conjugations,* etc.) and Be Especially Careful with Irregular Verbs, Such as *To Eat* and *To Write*

The main part of any verb is called its stem. The infinitive is the generic, basic form of a verb. It is shown by putting "to" in front of the stem. For example, the infinitive form of *sleep* is *to sleep*. The stem is *sleep*.

When you conjugate a verb, you add endings to the stem to show differences in meaning. For some verbs, the stem has to change its spelling when endings are added (to avoid unpronounceable forms, most often).

Once again, the real trouble arises with irregular verbs. For regular verbs, all you need to do is remember some basic principles, which follow (see Rule 21). For irregular verbs, you'll have to memorize the forms. The good news is twofold, though. First, there are relatively few irregular verbs to memorize. Second, most likely you will already recognize these verbs and their forms, so all you'll be doing is learning the terms for words you already use all of the time.

Irregular verbs are verbs for which the root word must be altered to form the past tense. The most notoriously irregular verb is *to be*, which when conjugated takes these various forms: *am, is, are, were, will be, is being, has been*.

EXAMPLES:

Present	Past Tense	Past Participle
begin	began	begun
break	broke	broken
choose	chose	chosen
do	did	done
eat	ate	eaten
drink	drank	drunk
fly	flew	flown
go	went	gone
shrink	shrank	shrunk
take	took	taken
write	wrote	written

For some verb tenses (see Rule 21), you use a helping or auxiliary verb, which appears before the main verb itself. These verbs are generally forms of the verbs *to be*, *to have*, and *to do*.

21. Know Your Verb Tenses: Past, Present, and Future

Verb tenses represent time. They indicate when an action, event, or state of being took place, and show its relation to when 'the words about that action, event, or state of being were written. To make your meaning clear, it is crucial that you know your verb tenses and use them correctly.

VERB TENSES

Present
Present Perfect
Present Progressive
Present Perfect Progressive

Past
Past Perfect
Past Progressive
Past Perfect Progressive

Future
Future Perfect
Future Progressive
Future Perfect Progressive

1. The present tense refers to the here and now. In the first and second person, it simply consists of th main stem of the verb; in the third-person sing the stem takes an -s ending. Irregular verbs, l verb *to be*, have to be memorized. Since *to be* is often used as a helping verb, its forms are listed below.

EXAMPLES: Mr. Ooze *looks* at the sky. Then he *walks* along, and *stares* at the trees, and he *thinks* about how green they *are*.

To be, present tense: I am   we are
                             you are
                             he/she/it is   they are

2. The *past* tense shows what happened at some earlier time. It is usually formed by adding *-ed* to the verb stem. Of course, irregular verbs have their own forms. The form with the *-ed* added is known as the past participle (for more on its use, see Rule 49).

EXAMPLES: Mr. Ooze *walked* along. He *watched* some birds with so much attention that he *forgot* to watch his step, and he *fell* in a big hole.

To be, past tense: I was   we were
                          you were
                          he/she/it was   they were

3. The future tense refers to events that have not happened yet, but that are expected to occur later in time. It is formed by putting the future form of *to be* before the stem of the main verb.

EXAMPLES: Mr. Ooze *will escape* from the pit he fell into. Still, he's afraid that it *will take* a long time.

To be, future tense: I will/shall   we will/shall
                                     you will
                                     he/she/it will   they will

Note that *shall* is an alternate form of the first person for the verb *to be*. It is used rarely in contemporary American English, but it is much more common in British English. Originally, *shall* was the normal form of the first person future, and *will* was used to add emphasis. Today, however, that distinction has largely been dropped, and using *shall* adds a note of formality. It is perfectly correct, though. It can also be used whenever *will* is being used as a helping or auxiliary verb, but again, it might seem a bit formal.

Helping or auxiliary verbs are forms of the verbs *to have*, *to do*, and *to be* (including such forms as *have*, *has*, *am*, *are*, *been*, *can*, *could*, *may*, *might*, *shall*, *should*, *will*, *and would*). They are placed before other verbs to help create various tenses and verb forms.

4. The present perfect tense combines the present tense with the past tense, to indicate that an action began in the past but has not ended, and is continuing in the present. It is formed by using the present tense of the auxiliary *to have* (I have/he has) before the past participle of the main verb (the *-ed* form).

EXAMPLE: Mr. Ooze *has walked* for a long time.

5. The past perfect tense shows when something happened further in the past, before something else. It is also known as the pluperfect. It is formed by putting the auxiliary *had* (the past tense of *to have*) before the past participle (the *-ed* form).

EXAMPLE: After Mr. Ooze *had walked* for a whⁱ
                 he saw some odd-looking birds.

To be,
past perfect tense: I had been   we had been
                       You had been
                       he/she/it had been they had been

6. The future perfect tense refers to things that have not happened yet, but that are expected to be completed later in time. It is formed by using *will have* as an auxiliary before the past participle (the *-ed* form, see Rule 49).

EXAMPLE: Mr. Ooze is determined to escape from his pit. It is deep, but by morning he *will have climbed* out.

7. The present progressive tense is what you use to show what you are doing on a continuing basis, not just at the moment. It is formed by using the verb *to be* as an auxiliary, and adding *-ing* to the verb stem. The form with the *-ing* added is known as the present participle (for more on its use, see Rule 49).

EXAMPLE: Mr. Ooze *is walking* along, and he *is looking* up at the sky. Unfortunately, he *is watching* the birds too intently.

8. The past progressive tense shows something that happened in the past, on a continuing basis. It is formed by using the past perfect form of the verb *to be* as an auxiliary before the present participle of the verb (the *-ing* form).

EXAMPLE: Mr. Ooze *had been walking* for hours, when he saw the birds flying upside down.

9. The future progressive tense refers to events that will be taking place, on a continuing basis, at some point in the future. It is formed by using *will be* as an auxiliary before the present participle of the verb (the *-ing* form).

EXAMPLE: That pit is so deep, Mr. Ooze *will be climbing* for quite a while to get out. He must be pretty mad at himself for forgetting about it, since he dug it in the first place.

10. The present perfect progressive tense refers to events that continue from the past into the present or beyond, into the future. It is formed by using both the present tense of *to have* (have or has) and the past participle of *to be* (been) as auxiliaries before the present participle of the main verb (the *-ing* form).

EXAMPLE: Mr. Ooze *has been climbing* for hours.

11. The past perfect progressive tense refers to events that continue in the past, and which had begun before some specific event, time, or situation. It is formed by using *had been* as an auxiliary (the past tense of *to have* + the past tense of *to be*) before the present participle of the main verb (the *-ing* form).

EXAMPLE: Mr. Ooze *had been climbing* for three hours before he got out of the pit. If only the sides hadn't been so steep!

12. The future perfect progressive tense refers to actions or conditions that will end by or at a specific time or moment. It is formed by using *will have been* as a compound auxiliary, followed by the present participle of the main verb (the *-ing* form).

EXAMPLE: If he's not out before then, by sunrise Mr.
Ooze *will have been climbing* for eight
whole hours.

EXERCISE

Identify all of the different tenses Mr. Ooze uses in
the following passage, and fix any mistakes he
makes. Remember that he has a very limited vocabulary, and these rules are still new to him.

I was walking. I saw birds. I fell. I hate that pit. I
hate those birds. Birds laughed; I know. I aching.
I will climb. I have been climbing all night. I will
escaped pit. I will walk. I will be watch path. I will
return. I will catch those birds. I will laugh.

22. Know That Adjectives, Such as *Tiny* and *Blue*, Describe Nouns or Pronouns

Now it's time to broaden Mr. Ooze's vocabulary by exploring descriptive words known as adjectives. Adjectives are words that describe, or modify, nouns and pronouns. They are useful because they allow us to explain how things appear to our senses, to tell things apart, and in general to add color to our lives. However, an adjective cannot stand alone in a sentence; it requires both a subject and a verb in order to function.

ADJECTIVE WITH NOUN: *fat* cat.

ADJECTIVE WITH NOUN AND VERB: is a *fat* cat.

The first example is missing a verb. In the second example, the subject is missing, since the noun *cat* acts as the object of the verb *is*.

CORRECT EXAMPLE: You have a *fat*, *fuzzy* cat.

Here, the words *fat* and *fuzzy* are adjectives, describing a particular cat. The sentence is now complete because it has a subject (*you*) and a verb (*have*).

Adjectives are essential to the English language because they present characteristics that help distinguish people, places, and things. Note how drab the following example is, when compared to the one after it.

DRAB: Mr. Ooze walked by the shore. He looked at the water. He watched the waves, and then saw the sun return to the skies.

COLORFUL: Mr. Ooze, a *handsome, athletic* man with *dark* hair, walked by the shore. His *narrow, bright* eyes squinted as he looked at the *gray* water. He watched the *high* waves, and then saw the *bright, vibrant* sun replace the *dark, cloudy* skies.

The second example tells you a lot more than the first one does. Now you have an idea what Mr. Ooze looks like, whereas at first he could have been anyone. You can visualize his activities by the water, notably *how* he looks upon it; you also have a clearer, sharper image of what kind of day it was (first cloudy and then sunny).

The trouble with adjectives is that they can be too powerful. Using too many isn't grammatically wrong, but it can suffocate your reader and make your sentences hard to understand. The second example above is certainly more interesting than the first one, but it also goes a little overboard.

EXERCISE

Mr. Ooze wants to show off and use some of his newly discovered words. Pick out all of his new adjectives.

I am handsome. I have brown eyes. I am strong. I dug that deep pit. I fell. I was hurt. Birds watched me. Those birds were mean. They crowed. Mean, ugly birds were loud. I will dig bird pit. It will be deep.

23. Be Familiar with the Functions of Articles, Such as *A, And*, and *The*

An article is a very specific kind of adjective. Remember that adjectives describe words; an article is used before a noun or a noun phrase to define or introduce it. That sounds intimidating, but in fact you use articles all of the time.

There are only three articles in the English language: *a, an*, and *the*. Now you know them all. *A* and *an* are called indefinite articles, because they show that you are talking about something that is singular, not plural, but not precisely defined. For example, if you said you saw *a* giant squid on the street, that just means that you saw one giant squid, possibly one of many, and no particular one at that. But if you said you saw *the* giant squid on the street, that means only one giant squid was there, and you saw it. *The* is called a definite article, because it defines a specific giant squid you saw. *The* can refer to things that are plural or singular; you could have seen *the giant squid*, or *the cars*.

The difference between *a* and *an* is that you use *a* before words that begin with consonants, and *an* before words that begin with vowels or vowel sounds (for example, words that start with silent *h*'s). If this sounds silly to you, try saying the phrase "a hour ago" rather than "an hour ago." Now *that* sounds silly. However, if the *h* is pronounced, such as in "historic," then one always uses the article *a*, as in "a historic landmark."

Articles can describe nouns, but they can also describe noun phrases. Several words grouped together can act as a noun; when that happens, they make up a noun phrase. For example, "the big, silly, furry cat" is a noun phrase; that collection of words describes a particular cat, and is indicated by the definite article *the*.

EXERCISE

As you will see, articles smooth out your sentences a great deal. Corroct Mr Ooze's attempts to use articles in the sentences below. Mark any noun phrases he uses as you edit the text.

I am a happy guy. An sun is shining, the day is wonderful. The wet grass is shiny. The sheep are funny. A bushes are tall. The sheep ate a bushes. The sheep ate tho wet, shiny, slimy grass. The sheep look green.

24. Recognize That Pronouns, Such as *Mine*, *Our*, and *Your*, Can Act as Adjectives

The very first rule in this book states that, depending on how they are used, words can often represent different parts of speech in different sentences. One of the most common changes occurs when pronouns act as adjectives.

This makes some sense, since after all, pronouns stand for other words in a sentence. They are there to help avoid repetition, but, depending on what kind of pronouns they are, they can also add more information about the word they are replacing in the first place. Since they are now describing the original word, they are acting as adjectives.

For example, the possessive form of personal pronouns can often act as an adjective. If I say, "that book is mine," *mine* is a personal pronoun, but it is also describing the book in question, so in that sense it is acting as an adjective.

EXERCISE

Underline any pronouns acting as adjectives in the following sentences.

My boyfriend's back.
Let go of our Eggos.
I left my heart in Moose Jaw, Saskatchewan.
Your liverwurst has a first name.

25. Know How to Form Comparative and Superlative Adjectives, Such as *Fine, Finer, Finest*

When you want to compare two things, use the comparative form of an adjective. You are saying that while something has a certain quality to it, a second person or object has more or less of that quality.

You generally create the comparative by adding *-er* to the root of the adjective (known as the positive degree). Sometimes, such as when a word ends in *e*, you simply add an *r*. Other times, if the word ends in *y*, change the *y* to an *-er*.

EXAMPLES: I am *tall*, but you are *taller*.
He is *cute*, but Mr. Ooze is *cuter*.
The birds are *happy*, but the sheep are *happier*.

Of course, keep in mind that quality could refer to when someone is lacking in something. In such cases, the comparative indicates that the second has even less. For example, if I didn't have very much money, but you had even less, I would be *poor*, but you would be *poorer*.

If you are comparing three or more things, use the superlative form. The superlative is usually formed by adding *-est* to the end of an adjective. As with the comparative form, if the word already ends with *-e*, you just add *-st*, and if it ends in a *-y*, you change the *y* to an *i* and then add the *-est*.

EXAMPLES: I am *tall*, you are *taller*, Peggy is *tallest*.
The writer is *cute*, the actor is *cuter*, but
Mr. Ooze is *cutest*.
The birds are *happy*, but the sheep are
happier, and the cats are the *happiest* of
all.

The biggest trick to remember is that you can't use
superlative terms when you are comparing fewer
than three things. If you have two apples, one of
them is tasty and one is tastier. You can't say that
one of them is tasty and the other one is tastiest,
because that implies that somewhere there's a third
one you haven't mentioned, which is the medium
tasty one. For more about comparatives and superlatives, see Rules 26, 97, and 98.

As is so often true with English, you have to stay on your guard for irregular forms, in this case comparative or superlative adjectives. Once again, there aren't that many irregular forms, but they tend to occur in very common words.

Two of the most common irregulars are the familiar qualitative pair of *good* and *bad*. Here are their forms.

Positive	Comparative	Superlative
good	better	best
bad	worse	worst

Then, of course, we have the quantitative pair, *more* or *less*. Here are their forms.

Positive	Comparative	Superlative
much, many	more	most
little	less	least

EXERCISE

Now that Mr. Ooze has some information on adjectives and how to compare things, he wants to share some of his opinions. Help him keep the comparative

53

and superlative forms straight — especially the irregular ones.

    I like animals. Sheep are good, dogs are more, cats are best. The bestest dogs find the lost sheep. The cats sleep. The dogs do the most, the cats do the less. I like to watch the cats climb the tall trees. They are the funnyest.

27. Know That Adverbs, Such as *Quickly* and *Heartily*, Describe Verbs, Adjectives, and Other Adverbs

Like an adjective, an adverb is another type of descriptive word. Adverbs modify verbs, adjectives, or other adverbs. If you want to describe how someone did something, you need to use adverbs.

EXAMPLE: Mr. Ooze ran *quickly* down the path. He heard the cat crying *piteously*, and he was very nervous. When he *finally* found the right tree, he couldn't help laughing *loudly*; there was Wesley, hanging *helplessly* between two branches like a furry orange hammock. After a few more moments of laughter, he reached up and pulled the cat down. Wes was *very* unhappy.

As you can see from the example above, most adverbs are formed by adding *-ly* to an adjective (if the adjective already ends in *-y*, you usually change the *-y* to an *-i* and then add the *-ly*). There are many exceptions, such as *very*, *much*, and *well*, but that's the basic rule.

EXERCISE

Turn these adjectives into adverbs.

sad	blind
happy	elated
listless	angry

28. Know That Most Negatives, Such as *None* and *Never*, Are Either Adverbs or Adjectives

Negatives are words that mean "no" or "not." They generally modify other words, negating or denying what is being stated, so they tend to be used as either adverbs or adjectives. For example, in the sentence "Mr. Ooze *never* comes home before eight," *never* is acting as an adverb, modifying the verb concerning Mr. Ooze's schedule.

A list of the most common negative words follows. You may recognize some of these words as indefinite pronouns (see Rule 12).

no	never
not	nothing
nobody	none

Be aware that negative words are often used in contracted forms (see Rule 79 on apostrophes). This generally is not considered acceptable in formal writing, however.

29. Know When to Use Comparative and Superlative Adverbs, Such as *More* and *Most*

Like adjectives, adverbs use comparative and superlative forms. In most cases, use *more* or *less* as an auxiliary before the adverb, to form the comparative, and use *most* or *least* the same way, to form the superlative.

EXAMPLE: Wes was Mr. Ooze's favorite cat. He'd run *more slowly* ever since he'd broken his leg, but that didn't bother Mr. Ooze. Wes was *less likely* to jump on the kitchen counter now.

Some adverbs follow the same rule as adjectives; you add *-er* to form the comparative and *-est* to form the superlative.

EXAMPLES: Of course, whenever he caused trouble, Wes could still run *faster* than Mr. Ooze, even though he was hardly the *fastest* cat on the block.

30. Be Careful of Irregular Comparative and Superlative Adverbs, Such as *Badly*, *Worse*, *Worst*

Unsurprisingly, not all adverbs follow the rules. Be careful of adverbs that have irregular comparative forms.

Here are some of the most common ones:

Positive	Comparative	Superlative
well	better	best
badly	worse	worst
little	less	least
much	more	most

Some of these forms should look familiar. Yes, they're the same forms as the adjectives, but now they appear as adverbs. This is another example of how the same word can often serve different functions depending on what part of speech it is.

EXERCISE

Underline all of the adverbs in the following passage.

Mr. Ooze walked slowly, planning his revenge against the evil, upside-down birds. He remembered vividly how they had crowed gleefully at

him, and he was absolutely determined that some-
day they would never crow again. He was still very
upset, but he tried to calm down and think more
rationally.

31. Know That Prepositions, Such as *In*, *Over*, and *With*, Show Relationships Between Words

Prepositions are nothing more than words that show relationships between other things or people in a sentence, such as direction, place, time, purpose, cause, and manner (the way things happen). They connect nouns with other nouns, verbs, or adverbs. Here is a list of common prepositions:

about	between	opposite
above	beyond	out
across	by	outside
after	down	over
against	during	past
along	except	since
among	for	through
around	from	toward
as	in	under
at	inside	until
before	like	up
behind	near	upon
below	of	with
beneath	off	within
beside	on	without

An old rule of thumb says that all of the words that describe where you could put something in relation to a table (on it, behind it, across it) are prepositions. This rule holds true, but bear in mind that some prepositions defy the rule, such as *inside*, *without*, and *since*.

Together with the nouns and other words that they control, prepositions make up what are called prepositional phrases.

EXAMPLE: Mr. Ooze put the book *on* the table.
Heather walked *toward* him.

In the first sentence, *on* is the preposition, and it governs the whole prepositional phrase *on the table*. This phrase tells you where Mr. Ooze put the book. In the second sentence, *toward* is the preposition, and it governs the prepositional phrase *toward him*. This phrase tells you which direction Heather was walking.

32. Remember to Use the Objective Case in Prepositional Phrases, Such as *For Me* and *With Us*

One good point about prepositions is that they are consistent about some things. For example, pronouns in prepositional phrases always take the objective case (see Rule 7).

EXAMPLE: The bear waited. Mr. Ooze walked toward *him*.

In the sentence above, *toward him* is a prepositional phrase (*toward* is the preposition) showing the direction Mr. Ooze is walking. The bear is the direct object toward which Mr. Ooze is walking, and so it makes perfect sense to put the pronoun in the objective case.

Unfortunately, this rule is quite commonly forgotten. People often say incorrect things like "Mr. Ooze had a good talk *with* the bear and *I*," instead of the correct ". . . *with* the bear and *me*." Many people who have been berated by English teachers about the objective case tend to panic and immediately choose the wrong pronoun without thinking it through; they assume *I* must be right because it has a formal ring to it. To avoid overcorrecting yourself and the use of *I*, remove the first object and say it out loud. The earlier sentence would thus read: "Mr. Ooze had a good talk *with*. . . ." Now separately add in the pronouns *I* and *me*. Clearly, "Mr. Ooze had a good talk with *I*" sounds clumsy and is, in fact, incorrect. By contrast, "Mr. Ooze had a good talk with *me*" sounds better because it incorporates the correct pronoun in the objective case.

33. Try Not to End a Sentence in a Preposition; If You Must, However, Go Ahead

One of the most famous "rules" in English grammar says that you should never end a sentence with a preposition. (This comes partially from the history of the word *preposition*, which literally means "word in front.") Unfortunately, there are times when to follow that rule you would have to break other, more important ones, such as "your sentences should make sense" and "don't use ridiculously complicated constructions." Sir Winston Churchill achieved grammarian immortality with his famous retort to this rule, "That is the sort of English up with which I will not put."

Fortunately, in these modern times grammar book writers are now allowed to speak the truth. Here is the new form of the rule: *Try not to end a sentence with a preposition. If you have to, though, go ahead.*

In other words, use common sense. If you can easily reword a sentence to avoid ending it with a preposition, and the new sentence is clear, fine. If, after several attempts, the new sentence remains complicated and ugly, give up. End with the preposition.

It is important to be aware of this rule, however, because there are still many professors and writers out there who prefer dogmatic rules to clear prose. Remember, you must know their rules before you can break them. It's one thing to break a rule knowingly and with reason; it's another to just blunder ahead blindly.

EXERCISE

Mr. Ooze wants to try out his prepositions. Identify the ones he uses, and correct any pronoun trouble he has.

I want to go boldly where I have never gone before. I will go back to the pit near the mean, upside-down birds. I will yell at the stupid birds. I will throw rocks at them. Mr. Ooze will laugh with Wes and I about them.

34. Know That Conjunctions, Such as *And* and *Until*, Connect Words, Phrases, or Clauses

Conjunctions are very useful words because they connect other words and even groups of words. You use conjunctions all of the time, whether you realize it or not.

There are four conjunctions that are used to connect words directly, plus three more that help out when needed. The basic conjunctions are: *and*, *but*, *or*, and *nor*. The conjunction *and* is sometimes helped by the word *both*. *Or* is often paired with *either*, and *nor* pairs up with *neither*. These two pairs can't ever be broken, by the way.

WRONG: It's *neither* yours *or* mine.

The rice, the shrimp *and* the sauce are *both* wonderful.

That's *either* fish *nor* fowl.

RIGHT: It's *neither* yours *nor* mine.

The rice *and* the shrimp are *both* wonderful.

That's *neither* fish *nor* fowl.

Conjunctions can also connect sentences, or parts of sentences. The ones listed above still work, but there are quite a few more that can only join groups of words (see Rule 36). Here is a list of the most common:

after	next
also	now
although	once
anyway	otherwise
as	since
as if	so
because	so that
before	still
besides	than
even though	that
for	then
furthermore	therefore
however	though
if	thus
indeed	unless
in order	until
instead	when
likewise	where
meanwhile	whether . . . or
moreover	while
nevertheless	yet

35. Know That Interjections, Such as *Oh* and *Wow,* Express Strong Feelings, but Do Not Affect the Grammar of a Sentence

An interjection is a word or phrase that is thrown into a statement, often as an expression of strong feeling. Since it is basically an interruption, it is grammatically unrelated to the other words in a sentence.

Almost any word or phrase can be used as an interjection, although naturally some are more common than others (and some are more printable than others). Sometimes a sentence will begin with an interjection, as the speaker or writer gets started. Other times, interjections will fall elsewhere in the sentence.

EXAMPLES: "*Oh*, you scared me!" Mr. Ooze said crossly to the bear.
"I was just walking along, minding my own business, and *whoops*, there you were. Sorry about that," the bear said.

In the first sentence, *Oh* is the interjection Mr. Ooze uses when he is frightened by the bear. In the second sentence, *whoops* is the interjection the bear uses to explain the sensation he felt when he suddenly encountered Mr. Ooze. In both cases, you could remove the interjection and the sentence would still make perfect sense. Note that interjectory sentences generally (but not always) end with exclamation points.

36. Know the Difference Between Phrases (Such as *The Big Moon*) and Clauses (Such as *The Moon Which Was Big*)

By now, you have become acquainted with all of the different parts of speech. If you remember that the same word can be identified as a different part of speech in any given sentence, depending on how it is used, you can identify just about any word in the English language. You also know your verb tenses and how to form them. Now it's time to start learning more about sentences and how they work.

First of all, it is important to understand the similarities and the differences between a phrase and a clause. Both of them are groups of words that can act as a part of speech in a sentence. For example, a noun phrase is a group of words that together act as a noun; there usually isn't a verb in such a phrase. A noun clause is a group of words that together can also act as a noun; but the difference is that clauses always contain verbs.

NOUN PHRASE: *The cuddly-looking cat* bit me.

NOUN CLAUSE: I thought *the cat was cuddly*, until it bit me.

As you recall, a sentence represents a complete thought (see Rule 17). Just as thoughts can be combined, so can sentences. If a sentence contains more than one group of words that could be a sentence on their own, those groups are known as clauses. In the example above, the clause *the cat was cuddly* could stand on its own as a complete sentence, since it has a subject and a verb.

Clauses are joined by conjunctions (see Rule 34), relative pronouns (see Rule 38), and sometimes by particular forms of punctuation (see Rules 65 and 67). They can be joined, or connected, in many ways, but can often exist on their own as sentences. They can perform several different grammatical functions, depending on how they are connected. Just as nouns and phrases can be subjects, direct objects, indirect objects, modifiers, or parts of prepositional phrases, so too can clauses.

SUBJECT: *The dog that barks* is starting to annoy me.

DIRECT OBJECT: I would like *the dog that barks* to shut up.

INDIRECT OBJECT: I'll give *the dog that barks* a piece of my mind.

PREPOSITIONAL PHRASE: The owner of *the dog that barks* must be hard-of-hearing.

Remember that parts of speech can change, depending on usage (see Rule 1). Both clauses and phrases can take on a variety of roles in different types of sentence constructions.

37. Understand the Difference Between Independent and Subordinate Clauses

When clauses are connected, two different types of clauses can be created. Sometimes they are joined in such a way as to remain equal; this means that if you broke them apart again, they would both still be complete sentences. However, sometimes one clause remains independent, while the other comes to depend on it for part of its meaning. It is now subordinate to, or dependent upon, the independent, or main clause. A sentence can have more than one dependent clause.

EXAMPLE: <u>Mr. Ooze was dozing quietly under a tree,</u> *when* suddenly his cat fell on him.

In the example above, the main clause is the underlined half of the sentence. Notice that it is a complete thought, with or without the following clause. The clause that begins with *when* is the subordinate clause. *When suddenly his cat fell on him* is not a complete sentence; the addition of the word *when* changes it from a complete thought to an incomplete one. In such cases, words like *when* are called subordinating conjunctions. Relative pronouns (see Rule 38) can also join subordinate clauses; then the subordinate clause is also known as a relative clause.

Not all conjunctions are subordinating ones, though. Conjunctions like *and* or *but* connect clauses directly, without subordinating one idea to the other.

EXAMPLE: Mr. Ooze woke up yelling, *and* the embarrassed cat ran off into the woods.

In the example above, both clauses remain independent. They are joined by the conjunction *and*, so they are each still complete thoughts.

EXERCISE

Connect the following clauses.

Mr. Ooze knelt over his sleeping wife. He bit her neck.

The match flared. The match sputtered. The match went out.

The burglar opened the window. Then she made her getaway.

38. Recognize Relative Pronouns, Such as *That* and *Which*

Relative pronouns connect subordinate clauses to the main clause of a sentence. When they do that, the subordinate clauses that follow them become known as relative clauses. A relative pronoun acts as a conjunction in that it links clauses of a sentence, and it acts as a pronoun in that its clause can be used to act as a part of speech.

The most common relative pronouns are: *that, what, whatever, which, whichever, who*, and *whoever*. *Who* and *whoever* are always used to refer to living creatures, *which* and *whichever* refer to things, and *that, what*, and *whatever* can refer to people or things.

EXAMPLE: The machine *that* made such a noise burst into flames.
He is one of those punks *who* tease my cat.
They are also the ones *who* glued together pieces of the puzzle.

In the first sentence, the relative pronoun *that* introduces a relative clause describing a noisy machine. In the second and third sentences, the relative pronoun *who* links relative clauses.

Like other pronouns, relative pronouns must agree with their verbs when they are used as subjects. This can get a bit tricky with *who*, since its antecedent can be either singular or plural. In the second sentence above, for example, *who* refers to the group of punks, not just one of the gang; thus, the verb *tease* is in the plural, not the singular.

EXERCISE

Insert the correct relative pronouns.

The cuttlefish _____ got away from Mr. Ooze is quite relieved.

There goes the octopus _____ borrowed my knitting needles.

They are the vampires _____ robbed the blood bank.

39. Know Which Case to Use in a Relative Pronoun Clause, Such as *The Guy Who Knows Everything*

Relative pronouns may have special duties in introducing relative clauses, but that doesn't exempt them from the rules of agreement. They must still agree with their verbs, and they must also maintain the correct case. This can be tricky, so keep in mind that the case of a relative pronoun is determined by its function in its own clause.

EXAMPLE: I threw a rock at the English teacher *who* was running away.

If you didn't know how to determine what case relative pronouns should be in, you might think that here *who* should be in the objective case, since it refers to the teacher *at whom* I threw the rock. But you are saved from this error by knowing the rule. *Who* is the subject of the dependent clause that describes the wise teacher, "*who* was running away," and so it belongs in the subjective case.

EXERCISE

Combine the following sentences, using relative pronouns. Make sure the pronouns agree and are in the correct case.

Cindy smiled at Hal, the talking bear. Hal looked uncomfortable.

Cindy's husband twisted his napkin. The napkin cried out.

Julia poked her Jell-O. The Jell-O wiggled reluctantly.

40. Know the Three Types of Sentences: Simple, Compound, and Complex

Basically, there are three kinds of sentences. They are defined by how complicated they are. If a sentence has only one clause, it is called a simple sentence. If the sentence contains two or more independent clauses, it is called a compound sentence. The clauses making up a compound sentence are called coordinate clauses. If a sentence contains a main clause and one or more subordinate clauses, it is called a complex sentence. These divisions cover every possible sentence in the English language.

SIMPLE: Mr. Ooze was angry at Wes. Cats were supposed to be graceful. Wes could not have fallen on him. Wes must have jumped. What a rotten cat.

The example above shows several simple sentences. None of them have more than one clause.

COMPOUND: At first Mr. Ooze was angry at the cat, *but* then he thought better of it. Cats were supposed to be graceful, *but* Wes had always been clumsy. Most of the time he was a good cat, *and* he knew how to program the VCR.

In this example, there are several compound sentences. The first two are both joined by the conjunction *but*, and the third is joined by the conjunction

78

and. All of the clauses remain independent; you could break any of the sentences in half and you would create two complete sentences, rather than incomplete ones.

COMPLEX: After a few minutes, Mr. Ooze began to feel guilty about having yelled *when* the cat fell out of the tree. He remembered the embarrassed way Wes had slunk off into the woods *while* he hollered. He was suddenly afraid that he had driven the little guy away, *even though* he hadn't meant to.

In this example, all of the sentences are complex. Notice that, despite their name, complex sentences need not be hard to understand. Each one simply contains a main clause and at least one subordinate clause. You can tell that they are not compound sentences, because in each case, the clause that begins with the subordinating conjunction is no longer a complete thought.

41. Be Familiar with the Three Types of Subordinate Clauses: Adverbial, Adjective, and Noun

One of the interesting things about clauses is that they can fill different functions in different sentences, depending on how they are connected. Subordinate clauses can be divided into three main groups: adverbial, adjective, and noun.

Adverbial clauses take over the function of a plain old adverb, by using an entire clause (instead of just one word) to qualify the action of the main verb of the sentence.

EXAMPLE: _While Wes slept under the shade of a fern_, Mr. Ooze walked through the forest looking for him.

In the example above, the underlined adverbial clause tells you when Mr. Ooze was walking; it was during the time Wes was sleeping. (For more uses of adverbial clauses, see Rule 42.)

Adjective clauses work in much the same way, using a clause instead of just an adjective to describe a noun or pronoun. They are generally relative clauses, introduced by either a relative pronoun or the relative adverbs _when_ or _where_ (see Rule 38).

EXAMPLE: The spot _where_ Wes was sleeping was so well hidden Mr. Ooze walked right by without seeing it.

In this example, the underlined adjective clause describes the cat's napping spot.

Noun clauses use a subordinate clause to serve as a noun in a sentence. They are usually introduced by *that* or *whether*. *That* is a relative pronoun, while *whether* is a conjunction.

EXAMPLE: Mr. Ooze didn't know *that* Wes was so close by until he stepped on his tail.

In this example, the noun clause introduced by *that* tells you what Mr. Ooze didn't know.

42. Use Adverbial Clauses, Such as *If She Arrives* and *As You Like*, to Express Time, Place, Manner, Degree, Comparison, Purpose, Result, Condition, Concession, and Cause

Adverbial clauses can convey many types of information. Remember, since they are clauses, they use an entire clause (rather than an adverb alone) to modify, or describe, a verb. They tell you a lot about the action of a verb, such as when its action occurs (time); where its action occurs (place); and how the action occurs (manner). They also express more abstract ideas, such as degree, comparison, purpose, result, condition, concession, and cause. Examples of each sort of use follow.

TIME: *When* I've finished working, we will go to the movies.

PLACE: The theater *where* the movie is playing is far away.

MANNER: We're not quite sure *how* we're going to get to the theater.

DEGREE: The theater is *very* far away.

COMPARISON: I hope this movie is better *than* the last one I saw.

PURPOSE: We want to go soon, *so that* we can be sure to get good seats.

RESULT: The reviews were so good *that* the theater is sure to be crowded.

CONDITION: *If* we're late, we'll have to sit apart.

CONCESSION: *Even if* it is crowded, we'll have a good time.

CAUSE: *Since* there were so many people, we wound up sitting in the front row.

As you can see in the above examples, adverbial clauses can be placed anywhere without changing the meaning of a sentence. Noun and adjective clauses, on the other hand, can mean different things depending on their placement in the sentence order.

43. Be Familiar with the Functions of Noun Clauses, Such as *The Car That Is Parked* and *The Person Who Wins the Race*

Since a noun clause takes the place of a noun in a sentence, it can do all of the things that a noun can. You can use a noun clause as the subject of a sentence, the direct object of a verb, an appositive (see Rule 44), a predicate nominative, or the object of a prepositional phrase. Remember that noun clauses often begin with a relative pronoun.

SUBJECT: *Why the cat fell out of the tree* is unknown.

DIRECT OBJECT: Mr. Ooze reported *that the cat fell out of the tree.*

PREDICATE NOMINATIVE: Wes is *the cat who fell out of the tree.*

OBJECT OF A PREPOSITIONAL PHRASE: He yelled *at the cat who fell out of the tree.*

44. Know That Appositives, Such as *Frosty the Snowman* and *Carrie, My Roommate,* Amplify or Explain the Meaning of the Noun to Which They Refer

An appositive is a noun or noun phrase that is put next to another noun or pronoun to amplify its meaning. Sometimes, a word may not give enough information, so more words are added to make the sentence clearer. These explanatory words are called an appositive, or they are said to be *in apposition to* the original word.

EXAMPLE: Mr. Ooze said, "Wes, *my cat*, is an idiot."

Here, the noun phrase *my cat* is in apposition to the name Wes, as it provides important further information. For example, you might not know that Mr. Ooze has a cat named Wes, so without the noun phrase you might think he was insulting some random person named Wes. By adding the appositive, his meaning becomes clear; he is not talking about any old Wes, but about the Wes who is his cat.

Remember, also, that since noun clauses can act as nouns in sentences, they can also act as appositives. For example, in the sentence "the news *that the cat had fallen* was not a surprise," the italicized clause adds information about, and thus is in apposition to, "the news."

45. Put Appositives in the Same Case as the Word to Which They Refer

For the sake of clarity, put appositives in the same case as the word to which they refer. This rule matters most when you are using either pronouns or a noun clause in apposition, since that is generally when case arises as a concern.

EXAMPLE: Mr. Ooze looked at all of us, <u>Wes, the bear, and *me*.</u>

In the sentence above, the underlined noun phrase is in apposition to the word *us*, since it explains who *us* is referring to. Since us is the direct object of the sentence, the noun phrase that is in apposition to it must also be in the objective case. You can tell that it is, since the pronoun *me* is in the objective case.

EXERCISE

Underline the appositives, and make sure any pronouns are in the correct case.

Padraic, the pirate, swashbuckled listlessly in the hot summer sun.
I'd rather eat a box of salt cod than my daughter Janie's homemade fudge.
Hal looked longingly at them, the dark ripe berries that he had been dreaming about for weeks.

46. Always Put the Subject of an Infinitive in the Objective Case as in *He Likes Me to Sing*

Infinitives can be used as nouns, adjectives, or adverbs. When infinitive phrases are used as the objects of verbs, the subjects of those phrases must also be put in the objective case. Again, you only tend to notice this when pronouns get involved.

EXAMPLES: I asked Mr. Ooze to move.
I asked *him* to move.

In both of the above sentences, Mr. Ooze is the subject of the infinitive, to move. In the second example, when Mr. Ooze is replaced by a pronoun, it must be in the objective case.

EXERCISE

Fill in the appropriate pronouns.

Mr. Ooze asked Wes to catch a mouse. Mr. Ooze asked _____ to do it quickly. Wesley told _____ to go away, because he was busy sleeping.

47. If You Can, Avoid Split Infinitives, Such as *To Lightly Tread*

Another of the most infamous rules in English grammar says that you must never split your infinitives. Since an infinitive is formed from two words, *to* + the verb, this rule means that you should never put another word between the *to* and the verb.

Like the rule stating that sentences should never end in prepositions, this one takes a good idea and pushes it too far. The problem with it is that there are times when it would simply be hideously awkward *not* to split your infinitives. Modern grammarians have finally faced this inconvenient fact, and so the new rule says: *Avoid split infinitives, but not slavishly*.

Probably the most well known split infinitive in American pop culture occurs in the introduction to the 1960s television program, "Star Trek." Our heroes' mission is set out clearly: *"To boldly go* where no man has gone before." (This was updated to the less sexist "where *no one* has gone" in films and in the 1980s–90s spinoff "Star Trek: The Next Generation." However, the split infinitive remained.) Now, try rewording that to avoid splitting the infinitive. "To go boldly where no man has gone before." "Boldly to go where no man has gone before." Both of these sound awkward, if not downright confusing. The original form conveys a certain sense of adventure and excitement that more "correct" phrasings could not carry.

This does not mean that you should split your in-

finitives whenever you get the chance. It does mean
that you should look carefully at any sentence where
you are using an infinitive, and think carefully about
the best way to express your meaning. If, after trying
to reword it, you decide that you have to split your
infinitive, go ahead.

48. Know When the *To* in an Infinitive Should Be Dropped, as in *I Dare Not Jump*

Just to confuse matters, there are some verbs that require you to drop the introductory *to* in an infinitive. In several cases, this occurs only in negative statements. Again, this is the sort of thing you do all the time, without even realizing that you are doing it.

EXAMPLE: I can *do* that. (I am able *to do* that.)
  You need not *raise* your voice. (You don't need *to raise* your voice.)

In the sentences above, the reworded versions in the following parentheses show the omitted *to*. Now, go back and try reading the sample sentences, and put the *to* in them; they sound (and are) incorrect. Use this as your test if you are ever unsure if a verb should be followed by the full infinitive form or not.

EXERCISE

Cross out any unnecessary "to's."

Wes would like to kill a mockingbird.
He need not to excuse his feelings; he's a cat.
Mr. Ooze dared not to stop him.
He must to do what a cat must to do.

49. Use Participles, Such as *The Frozen Lake* and *The Painted Car*, as Adjectives

Verbs have two forms which are called participles. The past participle is formed (in most cases) by adding *-ed* to the stem of the verb. The present participle is formed by adding *-ing* to the stem of the verb. (You will probably recognize both of these from Rule 21.) Both participle forms can be used as verbs, or as adjectives.

When the past participle is used as a verb, it shows that the action of the verb was performed at some time in the past. However, it can also be used as an adjective, describing a noun or pronoun.

EXAMPLES: I *knitted* a sweater.
Look at the *knitted* sweater.

In the first sentence, the participle *knitted* is being used simply as the past tense of the verb *to knit*. In the second sentence, however, it is being used as an adjective, to describe a particular sweater.

When the present participle is used in its verb form, it is called a gerund, and follows certain rules (see Rule 50). When it is used as an adjective, it describes nouns or pronouns.

EXAMPLE: The *falling* cat yowled.

In the above sentence, *falling* is the present participle. It is being used as an adjective, to describe the klutzy cat.

50. Use Gerunds, Such as *The Mixing of Ingredients* and *The Falling of Snow*, as Nouns

A gerund is the name of the present participle when it is being used as a verbal noun (see Rule 49); it is formed by adding *-ing* to the main stem of a verb. When you use a gerund as a noun, it does all of the things nouns can do; it can be the subject of a sentence, the object of a sentence, or the object of a prepositional phrase. A gerund can also have its own object.

EXAMPLE: *Baking* can be very satisfying. (subject)
I enjoy *baking*. (object)
Most people like the smell <u>of baking bread</u>. (object of the preposition *of;* <u>of baking bread</u> is the prepositional phrase)
Unfortunately, I hate *baking* bread. ("bread" is the object of the gerund *baking*)

EXERCISE

Gerunds can make your writing clearer and more concise. Use as many gerunds as possible and eliminate unnecessary words in the following sentences:

Everybody likes the way that Susan sings.
To go ride her bicycle is Janice's favorite pastime.
To fly is the quickest way to go to Boston.

51. Use the Possessive Case, Such as *Her Bowling Skill* and *My Baking*, to Modify Gerunds.

The only tricky thing to keep in mind about gerunds (other than what they are, of course) is that you should use the possessive case to modify them. You probably do this anyway, but you probably never thought about why you do it.

EXAMPLE: Mr. Ooze tried to improve his *speaking*.

In this sentence, *speaking* is the gerund; since it is acting as a noun, it demands that the pronoun referring to it be possessive. Mr. Ooze is trying to improve something that belongs to him, and so you refer to that something as *his*.

EXERCISE

Fill in the correct pronouns in the following sentences.

Mr. Ooze looked at _____ snickering cat.
He thought that perhaps Wes had been working on _____ mouse-hunting technique again.
Hal watched the two of them, and thought _____ laughing was very mean.

52. Know the Difference Between the Active Voice (Such as *Mr. Jones Bought Stamps*) and the Passive Voice (Such as *Stamps Were Bought by Mr. Jones*)

English has two voices, active and passive. The difference between them is simple, but important.

In the active voice, the subject of the sentence performs some sort of action, often on or to some object.

ACTIVE VOICE: Mr. Ooze shot the bird.

In the passive voice, the object of the sentence receives the action. It is formed by using the verb *to be* as an auxiliary before the main verb. The subject can often be omitted, or added as part of a prepositional phrase.

PASSIVE VOICE: The bird was shot [by Mr. Ooze].

The active voice is usually more direct and less wordy, so in terms of clarity and brevity it is generally preferred to the passive voice. Indeed, today there is such a strong presumption in favor of the active voice that you should be aware that some computer grammar checkers will *always* flag the passive voice as being a mistake. This is wrong. Don't be bamboozled by the old "the computer must be right" fallacy. This is a question which can only be answered on a case-by-case basis — by a human.

There are some instances where you simply can't use the active voice. For example, you may not know who shot the bird, or it may not matter. You could fudge, with something like "Someone shot the bird," but this might confuse your reader. It would be simpler to apply a passive construction. Using the passive voice also focuses attention on the object of the sentence, rather than on the subject, which is sometimes useful.

53. Be Aware of the Three Moods: Indicative, Imperative, and Subjunctive

Standard English has three moods: the indicative, the imperative, and the subjunctive. Most of what we say and write is in the indicative mood, because it signifies fact.

INDICATIVE: Mr. Ooze shot the bird.

The imperative mood is used for commands.

IMPERATIVE: Go shoot that bird.

The subjunctive mood is what we use to show that something is conditional, wishful, or contrary to established fact.

SUBJUNCTIVE: I wish that I had shot the bird.

Conditional forms are often signaled by the use of either *could* or *would*.

EXAMPLE: I *would* if I *could*.
I *could have danced* all night.

The subjunctive governs the realm of doubt, fantasy, and speculation. Sentences involving the subjunctive are often signaled by the words *if* and *that*. Instead of writing, "If Mr. Ooze was a woman," when he manifestly is not, you write "If Mr. Ooze *were* a woman." You would also use it in setting up a conditional statement: "If computers *were* simple, Mr. Ooze *would* be out of a job."

Although the subjunctive mood may seem confusing, it really isn't. In fact, since there are no exceptions lurking beneath the surface, subjunctive mood tenses should be easier to remember than other moods. Present-tense verbs do not change form in the subjunctive, no matter what: "It is important for you *to be* here." Note that the verb *to be* has not been conjugated. The past tense of *be* is always *were* in the subjunctive, no matter what: "If he *were* here, we'd be winning." And then there's the common phrase, "as it *were*." Since this mood often sounds strange to us, however, we are inclined to conjugate verbs and thereby make mistakes when using the subjunctive mood. Just stick to the no-conjugation rule and you won't have any difficulty.

EXERCISE

Identify which mood each of the following sentences is in.

"Catch that mouse!" yelled Mr. Ooze.
Wes looked lazily at Mr. Ooze, and continued licking his fur.
Mr. Ooze wished that Wes were not so annoying.
Wes thought that Mr. Ooze was very demanding.

54. Capitalize the First Word of a Sentence

Knowing the parts of speech and the rules that govern them isn't all there is to correct grammar. You also need to understand (and follow) the conventions that are used to write it all out, such as those concerning proper capitalization and punctuation.

Why do you need to worry about all of this? Capitalization and punctuation help people to figure out your intentions when you write, because they take the place of the physical cues you give when you are speaking. Part of why people speaking a foreign language sound as if they're speaking really fast is that if you don't know the words, you don't know where the breaks are between them. If someone spoke in a monotone, without ever pausing for breath, he or she would be very hard to understand, even if you were familiar with the language being used. Capitalization and punctuation show a reader where the breaks should go.

Capitalization begins by marking the beginnings of sentences. Always capitalize the first word of a sentence. Remember, too, that capitalization is used to separate proper nouns from common nouns (see Rule 3).

FIRST WORD OF SENTENCE: Can this be true?
Is your name really Mr. Ooze?
Yes, but you can call me Dan.

55. Capitalize Names, Titles, Places, the Pronoun *I*, and Words Referring to the Deity

In addition to proper nouns, there are certain specific words that should be capitalized. These include names of people, official titles, the pronoun *I*, and words referring to God. Be aware that titles should only be capitalized when they are used as such. When they are used as common nouns, they are not capitalized.

NAMES: Dan, Emily, Mr. Jones, Fred Smith

TITLES: Princess Diana, President Lincoln, Chairman Mao

BUT: The unhappy *prince* bemoaned his fate.

DEITY: God, His Son, Our Lord, Allah, Gaia, Yahweh, Zeus

PLACES: Madagascar, New York City, Nassau County

Also note that historic landmarks (the Statue of Liberty), legislative documents (the Bill of Rights) and product names (Adidas, Nike, Pepsi) should all be capitalized.

56. Capitalize Acronyms, Such as *RBI*, but Not Abbreviations, Such as *etc.*

Abbreviations and acronyms are both handy forms of shorthand for writers, but they follow different rules.

An acronym is made up of the first letter of each of the words in the name it stands for. An acronym is generally written with all of its letters capitalized and without periods separating letters.

EXAMPLE: the Culinary Institute of America = the CIA

or, perhaps better known,

the Central Intelligence Agency = the CIA

An abbreviation is a shortened form of the word being referred to itself. It usually ends with a period, and is generally not capitalized.

EXAMPLE: cup = c.

editor = ed.

ounces = oz.

57. Follow the Rules of Capitalization

There are some writers who think that it will add originality to their work if they ignore the rules of capitalization. Although they're perfectly willing to punctuate normally, they seem to think that the rules of capitalization are optional.

This is as wrong-headed as thousands of artists wearing an all-black uniform as a protest of nonconformism. The rules of capitalization exist to make it easier for readers to understand what you are trying to say. If you fail to capitalize a formal name and title, you may actually end up insulting the person being discussed. By deliberately putting a capital letter at the beginning of your sentence, you send a signal to your reader. Even e. e. cummings, who is perhaps best remembered for his experiments with capitalization and punctuation, limited such experiments to his poetry.

EXERCISE

Replace all the capital letters missing from the paragraph below (and notice how much harder it is to understand without the capitals).

as mr. ooze walked along the streets of the town, he was amazed by all the people who seemed to want to sell him things. he kept seeing words for many new things, like coca-cola, and he longed to ask what they were. however, he couldn't seem to make people understand him. this was frustrating, and after some time he found himself wishing that he were back in his cave by the lake. he was also frightened, and he was afraid that god had become angry at him.

58. Use a Period to End Declarative and Imperative Sentences (*Come Here.*), After Abbreviations (*Mrs.*), and to Indicate Decimals (*98.6°*)

Punctuation marks are crucial to written speech. They tell the reader where to pause or breathe, and they also differentiate among various kinds of statements. Periods are perhaps the strongest form of punctuation; you use them to end declarative and imperative statements.

EXAMPLES: Mr. Ooze cleaned his kitchen.

He ordered his cat, "Stay off that counter."

You must also use a period after abbreviations (see Rule 56). However, remember that you do not use them after acronyms. You should also be aware that British English follows slightly different rules regarding periods, and often does not require them after abbreviations (including Mr).

When writing out numbers, you should use a period to indicate decimals. For example, if I buy a Miracle Slicer-Dicer for nine dollars and ninety-nine cents, that would appear as $9.99. If the figure is for a number that is less than one, you should usually precede the decimal point by the number zero, to avoid confusion (without it, someone could misread the decimal point as a spot on the paper, and misunderstand the number). For example, the price of a candy bar that costs sixty cents would be written as $0.60.

59. Use Commas to Separate Words in a Series, Such as *Apple, Ball, Cat, and Dog*

Few people have trouble knowing where to put periods in a sentence, because the rules are fairly cut and dried. Commas, however, are another story altogether. This is largely because a comma signals a pause, rather than the end of a thought. They are used to separate elements within a sentence, not to mark the end of a sentence or thought. Whether or not to pause is often a much more subjective question than whether or not to end. Unsurprisingly, there are many rules about when to use (or not use) commas.

One of the most basic uses of a comma is to separate words in a series.

EXAMPLES: Mr. Ooze bought chocolate candy, soda, and cake.

Mr. Ooze bought chocolate candy, soda and cake.

The only difference between these two sentences is that the first one uses what is known as the serial comma, and the second one doesn't. All this means is that when you have three or more items in a series, if you are using the serial comma you put a comma after all of the items in the list (except the final one, of course). If you are not using the serial comma, you omit the last comma.

Either form is acceptable, as long as you are consistent. There are times when the serial comma can be particularly helpful, especially in sentences that have several compound nouns. However, switching back and forth randomly between the two styles is confusing. Pick a style, and stick to it.

EXERCISE

Add commas as necessary.

Wes is big yellow and furry.
Mr. Ooze is suave debonaire rich and unavailable.
My car is shiny fast expensive and wrapped around the old oak tree.

60. Use Commas to Separate Elements of Places (*Delmar, New York*), Dates (*October 30, 1972*), and Numbers (*10,000 Maniacs*)

Commas are often important in the conventions of how we write out certain information, especially when numbers are involved. Use a comma to separate elements of places, dates, and numbers.

PLACE: Mr. Ooze is from Barrington, Rhode Island.

DATE: We were married on September 9, 1995. (In European style, this would be written as 9 September 1995; no comma is used.)

NUMBER: That diamond necklace cost more than $1,000,000.

Notice that in whole numbers, commas are used to indicate divisions of thousands (in other words, every three digits over). In European usage, periods or spaces are often used. Commas are not used in fractions or decimals.

EXERCISE

Insert commas as necessary.

Mr. Ooze went to Northampton Massachusetts. He arrived on August 11 1995 and was greeted with 1765 bottles of beer. The beer was extremely expensive; it cost $100000!

61. Use Commas After Introductory Phrases, Such as *If You Go* and *Since the War*

You should generally use a comma after introductory phrases. This often includes phrases that precede speech (see Rule 74). Some style books say that a comma should only follow long introductory phrases, such as dependent clauses, prepositional phrases, or participial phrases. However, deciding whether or not a given clause or phrase is long is an extremely subjective matter.

EXAMPLE: Once upon a time, there was an enchanted weasel.

The important thing to keep in mind is that you should be consistent. Do not put a comma after an introductory clause in one sentence, and then omit one in the very next paragraph.

EXERCISE

Decide where the commas should go.

In the beginning there was Mr. Ooze.
And now back to the Mr. Ooze Show. But first a word from our sponsor.
According to Wes Japanese VCRs are the best.

62. Use a Comma to Separate Independent Clauses Joined by Conjunctions, Such as *He Is Well, but He Looks Awful*

Since commas are used to separate elements in sentences, and to indicate pauses, you should generally use a comma to separate independent clauses joined by a conjunction.

In recent years, this rule has often been relaxed in cases where the clauses are considered short and simple enough for the meaning to be clear without a comma. Once again, though, the decision as to what is "simple" and "short" is quite subjective; the safe answer is to follow the traditional rule.

EXAMPLES: Mr. Ooze listened, but the noise was gone.

It was dark, and he was frightened.

EXERCISE

Insert commas as you see fit.

The apartment was dirty and it had no stove.
Mr. Ooze complained to the landlord but to no avail.
After a week he moved out.

63. Set Off Clauses That Are Not Essential to the Sentence with Commas, Such as *Joe, My Partner, Will Be Late*

You should set off a nonrestrictive clause, or one that is not essential to the sentence, with commas. Conversely, you should not set off a restrictive clause, or one that is essential to the sentence, with commas. Appositives, for example, are usually nonrestrictive, so they are generally set off with commas (see Rule 44).

Sadly, this is one of the most common sources of error in comma usage, even though it is easy to check. If you are unsure as to whether or not the clause or phrase in question is necessary to the meaning of your sentence, simply try reading the sentence without it. Does it still make sense? If so, the clause is not essential, so it is nonrestrictive. Thus, it should be set off with commas. If the sentence no longer makes sense, then the clause or phrase is necessary and thus restrictive, and should not be set off with commas.

EXAMPLES: The tea *on the desk* is getting cold, while the tea *in the pot* is still hot.

My ice cream, *which was sitting in the sun,* melted.

In the first sentence, the italicized phrases are necessary to distinguish the tea which is cooling from the tea which is not. They are restrictive, so they are not set off with commas. In the second sentence, it is

111

clear what has melted (my ice cream), so the information about it sitting in the sun is not essential to the meaning. That clause is nonrestrictive, and marked off by commas.

EXERCISE

Test the following sentences to see which clauses are restrictive and which are not. Insert commas as necessary.

The sports car with the large wheels is red.
Mr. Ooze with a look of awe touched the car's paint.
The owner of the car noticing Mr. Ooze honked the horn.
Mr. Ooze frightened by the horn ran away.

64. Use Commas to Clarify Ideas, Such as *She Wants to Go, Clearly, but She Can't*

As you can see, there are various rules that govern the use of commas. However, they cannot cover every eventuality. There are times when a sentence can be confusing, and a comma would help clarify matters. In such cases, use your common sense.

This is not meant to be a blank check for adding commas either. Too many commas can be as confusing as too few. Think about your sentences and what a comma would mean.

EXAMPLE: He came in, in a fury, and began shouting.

Here the first comma isn't strictly necessary, but it helps to avoid confusion with the double use of the word "in."

EXERCISE

Insert commas, with clarity as your goal.

Mr. Ooze had hoped that the car owner would appreciate his interest in the sports car but apparently he didn't.

He drove off in a huff quickly shifting into fifth gear.

Unfortunately he drove off so quickly he forgot to watch where he was going and he hit a building. The fancy car looked ridiculous stuck in the revolving door of the hotel.

65. Use Semicolons to Separate Independent Clauses, as in *We Came; We Saw; We Conquered*

In general, semicolons are used to signal stronger breaks in sentences than commas, but weaker ones than periods or colons. They often cause confusion, simply because of this rather "in-between" grammatical status. However, there are a couple of specific rules to help you know when to use them properly. One of them states that you should use a semicolon to separate two independent clauses not joined by a conjunction.

EXAMPLES: Mr. Ooze ran for a long time; he sweated a lot.

Mr. Ooze ran for a long time, *and* he sweated a lot.

Notice the subtle difference in meaning and tone between the two sentences above. In the first sentence, the semicolon marks a rather sharp pause between the two clauses. In the second, the emphasis has changed. Using a semicolon in such cases often emphasizes the link or the contrast between the clauses.

66. Use Semicolons to Separate Multi-Word Elements in Lists, Such as *Dogs and Cats; Men and Women;* and *Night and Day*

Semicolons can also be used to separate clauses or phrases that make up a list.

Note that they are *not* used to introduce the list; colons do that (see Rule 68). This is a common error. Instead, semicolons are used to separate the elements of a list when they are long or contain punctuation of their own, because in such cases commas would be confusing.

EXAMPLES: Mr. Ooze likes to eat chocolate, chicken glop, and uncooked pasta; Wes the cat likes to eat fish, chicken, and broccoli; and Hal the talking bear likes to eat berries, honey, and chicken-fried steak.

Notice how confusing the above sentence would be if you tried to replace the semicolons with commas.

EXERCISE

Insert semicolons wherever necessary and correct those that are misplaced.

Hal was hungry, it had been a bad summer for berries.

The evil birds had eaten them all everything, including the blueberries, strawberries, and even the blackberries.

What was a self-respecting bear to do; eat humans?

When in doubt; call Ghostbusters.

67. Use a Colon to Separate Independent Clauses That Explain One Another, Such as *He Went: Not Happily, but He Went*

Colons mark sharper breaks in sentences than either commas or semicolons. Like semicolons, they can be used to separate two independent clauses that are not connected by a conjunction. However, you use a colon to separate two independent clauses *when the second amplifies or illustrates the first.*

In practice, what does this mean? A colon tells the reader that the second clause has new information about the first clause. It also stresses the connection between the two independent clauses. When the second clause is a full sentence, it should begin with a capital letter. This reinforces the strength of the break (by contrast, a clause following a semicolon is never capitalized). If the second clause is merely a phrase, however, it should not be capitalized.

EXAMPLE: Mr. Ooze looked at the bear: It was awfully big and looked very hungry.

In the sentence above, the clause following the colon tells you more about the bear. Thus, it amplifies the meaning of the first clause.

68. Use a Colon to Introduce Lists (*The First Four Letters: A, B, C, D*) or Speech (*The Priest Bellowed: "Dearly Beloved. . . ."*)

The primary use for colons is to introduce lists or long quotations. Semicolons can break up the elements following the colon, if necessary, but they cannot be used to introduce the list in the first place (see Rule 66). Colons often precede speeches or dialogue as well.

EXAMPLES: Hal was so hungry that he began dreaming of all his favorite foods: chocolate, potato chips, pudding, and underripe blackberries.

Mr. Ooze addressed the crowd: "Yo, everyone. . . ."

Notice that colons can also be used to set off examples (as they do in this book).

EXERCISE

Make sure colons are used correctly in the following sentences.

Hal decided that something had to be done: if those rotten birds weren't stopped soon, everyone would starve.

He booked the biggest auditorium in town, and made a speech: "Friends, the birds are against all of us. What shall we do?"

After the speech, Mr. Ooze came up to talk to him and said, "I hate those birds too, for several other reasons: they're not just greedy, they're mean; they crowed at me when I fell in the Pit of Peril; and they fly funny."

69. Use a Question Mark to End an Interrogative Statement, Such as *Are You Serious?*

Like a period, a question mark generally signals the end of a complete thought. However, question marks are used only to end interrogative statements.

EXAMPLES: How do I do this?
What is your name?

Both of the sentences above are examples of direct questions. These are simple to punctuate, since they always require a question mark. Indirect questions, however, are trickier. These do not take a question mark at the end, since they are really statements about questions, rather than questions themselves.

DIRECT QUESTION: Mr. Ooze asked the bear, "Have you always known how to talk?"

INDIRECT QUESTION: Mr. Ooze asked the bear if it had always known how to talk.

Notice that when quotation marks are used, the question mark appears inside them (for more on the effects of quotation marks, see Rule 74).

70. Use an Exclamation Point to End an Exclamatory Statement, Such as *You're Joking!*

An exclamation point serves only one grammatical function: it is used to add emphasis. The only time you use an exclamation point is to end an exclamatory statement. For example, upon meeting Hal, someone might say, "Oh my goodness, that bear can talk!"

If an exclamatory statement is being quoted, then the exclamation point should go inside the quotation marks (see Rule 74). No other punctuation should follow it directly, even if a phrase identifying the speaker comes after it in the sentence.

CORRECT: "Oh goodness, a talking bear!" cried out Mr. Ooze.

INCORRECT: "Oh goodness, a talking bear!," cried out Mr. Ooze.

The trouble with exclamation points is that they are easy to overdo. Use them as sparingly as possible; if your writing is strong, you can make your meaning clear without them. Like profanity or strong language, exclamation points lose their power if they are used constantly.

EXERCISE

Rewrite the following paragraph, removing the unnecessary exclamation points.

After the big meeting, Mr. Ooze complained, "I hate crowds! They're so noisy and smelly and loud! And those teenagers sound so breathless, as though everything is so important! Sheesh!" Mr. Ooze hated the meeting!

71. Use Dashes to Indicate Interruptions in Thought, Such as *I Think—Actually, I Know—That I'm Hungry*

Dashes are used to signal a break in the writer's thought. They indicate an interruption that would disrupt the logic of a given sentence if it were not marked off in some way. In typesetting, long dashes are referred to as *em dashes*, since they are the width of a capital letter M. Many word processors have a key code that allows you to use a proper em dash. If yours does not, or if you are using a typewriter, use two hyphens next to each other.

EXAMPLE: Mr. Ooze was walking along, daydreaming about food—he wasn't actually hungry, it was more out of habit—when he fell in the pit again.

Dashes can also be used as a sort of shorthand, to connect clauses or phrases without linking words. They can be helpful, but they can also seem rather casual.

EXAMPLE: The typesetter has the instructions—I faxed them over yesterday—so he should know what to do.

Unfortunately, many people use dashes in place of proper punctuation: "Oh, I need a break of some kind here, and I don't want to bother my head about the rules regarding semicolons and colons and all, so I'll just throw in a dash." No one is fooled by this. Only use dashes when you are certain that they fit correctly. Do not replace specific punctuation marks with an elusive dash.

Hyphens are punctuation marks that are used within words. They are used when breaking words at the end of a line, joining compound adjectives or nouns, or joining prefixes that could otherwise cause confusion.

If there are too many words to fit on a given line of type, the last word is usually broken. This means that it is split into two parts, generally between syllables, and a hyphen is inserted after the first half, to indicate that there is more of the word on the next line. One-syllable words cannot be so broken, though, and you should avoid breaks that would put fewer than three characters on the next line.

EXAMPLE: Mr. Ooze listened to the polysyllabic professor droning on, and wondered idly why the woman couldn't manage to use shorter words.

Hyphens are also used to join compound nouns or adjectives. The question of when to hyphenate and when not to can be one of the most vexing (and

126

changeable) that writers face. In general, compound adjectives should be hyphenated when they appear before the word they are modifying, but they should not be hyphenated when they follow it.

EXAMPLE: Wes is a *six-year-old* cat.
Wes the cat is *six years old.*

Compound nouns tend to follow a distinct pattern of evolution. They begin as two separate words. As they become more commonly used, they are often hyphenated. Eventually, the hyphen disappears, and a new word is created.

EXAMPLE: kick stand
kick-stand
kickstand

The trouble, of course, is knowing what stage of word evolution a given compound noun is in. Here, the dictionary is your best friend. However, there are some compound nouns that you can be sure will remain hyphenated. These include fractions and the spelled-out numbers from twenty-one to ninety-nine. Some common compound nouns and adjectives:

anti-aging	sister-in-law
cross-stitch	six-shooter
double-dip	so-called
eye-opener	twenty-fifth
fire-breathing	well-dressed
ill-prepared	Stratford-upon-Avon

The last use of hyphens is for joining prefixes to words. Prefixes must be followed by a hyphen before a numeral, or a capitalized word, but they are also helpful in cases that could otherwise cause confusion.

EXAMPLES: In this *post-1984* world, Orwell seems to
have been too pessimistic.

Wes, despite being a cat, was *anti-
PETA*.

After his newly refinished floor was
damaged, poor Padraic had to *re-refinish*
it.

73. Italicize or Underline Titles of Books (*East of Eden*), Movies (*The Wizard of Oz*), Other Major Works (*The Nutcracker Suite*), Foreign Words (*Coup D'État*), and Emphasized Words or Phrases (*"We Will Not Be Undersold"*)

The word italic refers to a specific kind of typeface, which is generally slanted more than regular (roman) type. Italic type is used to set off the titles of books, movies, full-length plays, foreign words, and emphasized words or phrases. (If you are using a typewriter and cannot create italic type, underlining is considered its equivalent.)

EXAMPLES: Mr. Ooze's favorite book is by Casanova, *The Adventures of Don Juan*.
His favorite movie is *Sorority Babes in the Slimeball Bowl-a-Rama*.
They both exemplify a certain *je ne sais quoi*.

Italics can look quite sophisticated, and this can be rather seductive. Try to resist the siren song of fancy typography, however. Like most gimmicks, it loses force quickly when overused. Don't rely on italics to provide emphasis; make your writing strong on its own.

74. Use Quotation Marks to Enclose Direct Quotes ("*I Have a Dream*"), Slang ("*Way Cool*"), Titles of Essays ("*The Theme of Religion in the Bible*"), Short Stories ("*The Pit and the Pendulum*"), Poems ("*Jack and Jill*"), and Songs ("*The Battle Hymn of the Republic*")

Quotation marks are primarily used, as their name suggests, to enclose quoted material (they are also referred to simply as quotes). In such cases, they are only used to indicate direct quotations; if you are paraphrasing someone's remarks, you should not set them off in quotation marks. Quotes are also used to indicate slang (or any nonstandard word or phrase), and to set off the title of an essay, short story, poem, or song. Generally, names of television and radio programs should be in quotes. However, if one is also referring to specific names of episodes, it is then considered more acceptable to italicize the name of the show and place the episode name in quotes (e.g., "The Trouble with Tribbles" from *Star Trek*).

EXAMPLES: He asked, "Do you like to read?"
The teacher protested that she was not just "surfing the Net" for fun.

George Orwell's essay "Politics and the English Language" should be read by everyone who is interested in good writing.

Joyce's short story "The Dead" is perhaps his finest work.

I find Edgar Allan Poe's poem "The Bells" very annoying.

Her favorite song is "I Love You," by the Psychedelic Furs.

The real problem with quotation marks is the effect they have on other forms of punctuation. Some punctuation marks go inside the quotation marks, some go outside, and sometimes punctuation marks shouldn't appear at all. This causes a great deal of confusion, but the rules are actually fairly simple.

When quotation marks are used to set off a complete quote, all of the punctuation goes within the quotes.

EXAMPLE: Mr. Ooze said, "I'm going to go tease the bear."

However, when quotation marks are used to set off words for any other reason, sentence-ending question marks and exclamation points go outside the quotes.

EXAMPLES: I don't think you should go "bear-teasing"!

Do you really want to go "bear-teasing"?

When quoting a sentence, if the information describing the speaker comes in the middle, the first half should end with a comma inside the quotation marks, the identifying part should end with a comma, and then the final punctuation should fall within the quotation marks.

EXAMPLE: "You wimp," he shouted, "let's go!"

See also Rule 70 for what to do if a phrase identifying the speaker follows an exclamation.

Regular quotation marks are used to indicate direct quotation. However, sometimes you need to enclose a quotation within another quotation, or to set off a phrase within a quotation that would normally be enclosed by quotation marks. In such cases, you should use single quotation marks.

EXAMPLES: After he got out of the hospital, he told me, "Then she yelled, 'Get away from my bear, you idiot!' "

I said, "Well, you really shouldn't have gone out 'bear-teasing,' you know."

It is perfectly acceptable to have a single quotation mark appear next to double quotation marks (indeed, it happens frequently). As for the placement of punctuation, follow the same rules you do for regular quotation marks, as in the examples above (see Rule 74).

Note that in British writing single quotes are used the same way double quotes are in America.

EXERCISE

Punctuate the following sentences, making sure the quotation marks go in the right place.

Is bear-teasing as much fun as cow-tipping
Heather asked
Oh it is much more fun Mr. Ooze assured her I do
it all the time
My mother always told me bears could be danger-
ous she said doubtfully
I'd rather go cow-tipping she concluded

76. Use Ellipses to Indicate Incomplete Thoughts or Omissions from Quoted Material, Such as "*Most Physicians Recommend . . . Exercise*"

Ellipses are a series of three periods that are used to indicate incomplete thoughts or omissions from quoted material. When they appear at the end of a sentence, they are followed by a period, so you wind up with four periods in a row. They can also be followed by other punctuation, such as commas.

EXAMPLES: "Isn't the lake lovely, on such a day . . . ," said Mr. Ooze, his voice trailing off as his mind wandered.

"There are a half-a-dozen reasons why you should vote for me," began the candidate. "First, because . . . second, because I'm a nice guy . . . and finally, because I want the job. Thank you."

Booklist raved: "It stands as the best piece of literary fiction of 1995. . . ."

Ellipses are another handy tool that can easily be misused. It is not, strictly speaking, grammatically wrong to have all your arguments end by trailing off into nothingness, but if you are trying to actually say anything, it is a very bad habit. Worse, too many ellipses in quoted material can destroy your credibility, because it makes you look as though you are trying to change the original meaning of the quotation.

77. Use Brackets to Indicate Additions to Quoted Material, Such as "*He [Joe] Will Arrive Soon*"

Brackets serve the opposite function of ellipses; they are used to indicate additions to quoted material, rather than omissions. Most commonly, they are used to indicate a word or phrase that does not appear in the original quotation, but which the current writer considers necessary for understanding. This also occurs frequently in transcription or reports of conversations, since the reader may lack contextual information.

EXAMPLE: He [the housing dean] is a complete fool.

Sometimes brackets are used to add comments by the writer. This can be necessary, as in cases where there is an error in the original material. To avoid having readers think that the mistake was unwittingly copied (or created by the writer), the Latin phrase *sic* (meaning "so it was") is inserted, in brackets. More substantive comments can also be added, but it is usually better to finish the quotation and then comment.

EXAMPLE: The note from the housing dean read, "The redecoration of your cave will be soon be finished, liaising [sic] with Mr. Ooze as needed."

Parentheses are used to enclose supplemental material in a sentence. They can enclose an interruption or a comment, or any additional information that doesn't fit into the flow of the main sentence.

EXAMPLE: Hal warned Mr. Ooze (not that he ever listens, of course) about the pit on the path, but of course he forgot again.
Hal calls it the Pit of Peril, because it's really very deep (fifteen feet).

A note of caution: By definition, parentheses disrupt the flow of your thought. Thus, you should be careful not to use them too often. Parenthetical remarks can quickly become distracting when overused. If you find that you are relying on them heavily, see if you can find ways to fit the information directly into your sentence, setting it off with commas if necessary. Alternatively, ask yourself if it is really important to have the information in that sentence, or if it would go better elsewhere.

EXERCISE

Correct the use of parentheses in the following paragraph.

Hi, I'm Hal (the talking bear). I just wanted to say a few words (since it seems as though all you're hearing about me) has to do with eating berries (as if that were all I do). I'm much smarter than that. (Did you know that I'm a ranked squash player, a tiddlywink champ, and a major fan of magazine photography?) People think I'm just a big (hungry) bear, and that makes me mad.

79. Use Apostrophes to Represent Omitted Letters in Contractions, Such as *Can't* and *Weren't*

An apostrophe is the punctuation mark used to represent omitted letters, as when forming contractions. Remember that only one apostrophe is used, no matter how many letters are omitted.

EXAMPLES: I don't [do not] want to eat any more potatoes.
We had buckets o' fun at the movies.

Contractions are generally considered to be rather informal. They are quite common in spoken English, but they are rarely acceptable in formal written material. The only way to know whether or not they can be used in any given context is to ask someone in authority, such as your teacher, editor, or boss.

There are a few contractions that have been around for such a long time that they have become accepted as standard, formal English, such as "six o'clock" (from the now archaic "six of the clock"). In such cases, the original is no longer used. (For more on contractions, see Rules 99 and 100.)

EXERCISE

Make the following italicized word phrases into contractions:

Cannot you handle this problem while *I am* on vacation?

Let us go to the park on Sunday. *It is* supposed to be a beautiful day.

What is the matter with Harry? *He would* rather stay home than visit me. *Should not* I call to check on him?

The above sentences are informal in tone; they resemble casual conversation more than formal writing. In informal instances such as these, contractions may sound better than full words. However, in formal writing, you should avoid contractions since they often sound overly informal. Write out the full words from the following contractions.

It's become clear that *he'd* be a better candidate than Joe.

She'll notify you if *you've* been selected to announce the award.

The professor *should've* approached the trustees with her decision.

80. Use Apostrophes to Form Possessives (*Amy's Pen*), and the Plurals of Letters (*Two S's*), Numbers (*Two 10's*), and Symbols (*Two $'s*)

Apostrophes have two other uses: They are used to form possessives, and to create plural forms of letters, numbers, and symbols.

To indicate possession, add an apostrophe followed by an *s* to singular or collective words. The same is true for plural words that do not end in the letter *s*; for those that do, add an apostrophe but no final *s*. Personal pronouns (e.g., *her*), however, do not take apostrophes. Proper names that end in *s* take *'s*: Lois's raincoat; Jesus's words.

EXAMPLES: That is Mr. Ooze's book.
This is Charles's top hat.
Where is the college's squash court?
What are you going to do about that mass of spiders' nests?
But: This cat is hers [not her's].

You also use apostrophes to create the plural forms of letters, numbers, and symbols. This is generally done to avoid confusion.

EXAMPLES: Hal the bear got straight A's this year in English class. All his test grades were 99's or better.

142

81. Use Slash Marks to Separate Parts of Dates (11/24/70), to Replace the Word *Per* ($1.00/dozen), and to Separate Quoted Lines of Poetry or Songs in Text ("*For He's a Jolly Good Fellow/ Which Nobody Can Deny*")

A slash mark (also known as a virgule) should be used to separate parts of dates, to replace the word *per*, and to separate quoted lines of poetry in text. The first two uses are sometimes considered rather casual and informal, but the third is always acceptable.

EXAMPLES: His birthday was 9/21/66. (September 21, 1966)

This car gets 80 miles/gallon. (80 miles *per* gallon)

"Two roads diverged in a wood/and I, I took the one less traveled by/and that has made all the difference." ("The Road Not Taken," Robert Frost)

82. Know the Difference Between the Verbs *Set* and *Sit*

These words are often confused or used interchangeably, even though they have different meanings and usages. *Set* means "to place or position" and is generally followed by the prepositions *on, in,* or *under*. *Sit*, on the other hand, means "to take a seat," and is never followed by a preposition except the occasional *down*, as in *to sit down*. This construction is informal and should be avoided in proper writing.

One more distinguishing feature: *set* usually has a direct object, while *sit* never does. A person *sets* an object somewhere; but a person *sits* on a chair. To put a direct object after *sit*, as in *to sit one's buttocks* in a chair, would be unnecessarily repetitive and grammatically perplexing.

EXERCISE

Choose the correct verb in the following sentences.

Mr. Ooze would like to (set/sit) his hat down.
I would like to (set/sit) down for a while.
Natalie (sets/sits) her hands on her lap as she waits.
Bart's back hurt from (setting/sitting) in the car so long.

144

83. Know the Difference
Between the Verbs *Lay* and *Lie*

These two similar-sounding verbs are often confused because the past tense of *lie* is *lay*. *Lay* is a transitive (action) verb that means "to put down" or "to place lengthwise." It almost always takes a direct object, as in *to lay one's life on the line*. Other forms of the verb *lay* include *laid*, *laying*, and *laid*.

Lie is an intransitive (non-action) verb that means "to recline" or "to be located." The verb *lie* never takes a direct object; you can *lie* on the bed, but you cannot *lie your shirt* on the bed. *Lie* also appears in the forms *lay*, *lying*, and *lain*. The tricky part of keeping these two verbs separate in your mind is knowing that the past tense of *lie* is *lay*, as in *she lay on her bed yesterday*.

You'll remember the various usages and forms if you memorize these partial conjugations:

lay, laid, laying, laid
lie, lay, lying, lain

EXERCISE

Choose the correct form of the verb in the following sentences:

Mr. Ooze always says that the path to happiness (lays/lies) in your own heart.
Three babies are (laying/lying) in the crib.
The carpenters have (laid/lain) the basement and the ground floor of the new building.

84. Know the Difference Between the Verbs *Raise* and *Rise*

These two similar-sounding verbs are often confused because they look as if they might be two forms of the same verb, when in fact they are different verbs entirely. *Raise* is a transitive (action) verb that means "to set upright" or "to bring to a higher position." It must take a direct object, as in *to raise the sail*.

Rise is an intransitive (non-action) verb that means "to assume an upright position" or "to go higher." The verb *rise*, like most other intransitive verbs, does not require a direct object, as in *the balloon rises*. Much of the confusion comes from the similarity in pronunciation and meaning of the two verbs.

Both words exist in noun forms, but the noun *raise* refers exclusively to an increase in pay. The noun *rise* has many different meanings: the *rise* of the hills; a *rise* to power; a *rise* in the cost of living; and the informal denotation, to get a *rise* out of somebody.

EXERCISE

Choose the correct word in the following sentences:

We'll all melt if the temperature (rises/raises) much more.

There has been a (raise/rise) in the number of mallard ducks in the neighborhood pond.

Shawn (raises/rises) many excellent questions.

85. Know the Difference Between the Comparative Adjectives *Fewer* and *Less*

Fewer refers to things that can be easily counted and quantified by amounts such as numbers, weight, or time. *Less* refers to abstract measurements of things that cannot be counted.

In these sentences, note which objects can be enumerated and which are too general to be assigned numbers.

EXAMPLES: I have fewer marbles than I used to.

I have less of a grasp on reality now than when I was younger.

There are fewer hamburgers than hot dogs.

There is less food than necessary for the barbecue.

EXERCISE

Choose *fewer* or *less* in the following sentences:

There are (fewer/less) black keys than white keys on a piano.

Mr. Ooze would like to see (fewer/less) of the family that lives across the street.

Do you want more or (less/fewer) candies than I've taken.

(Fewer/Less) people travel in the autumn than in the winter.

86. Be Wary of Using the Verb Form *Got*

The verb "to get" can appear in the forms *get* (present tense), *got* (past tense), and *gotten* (past participle). *Got* can properly be used in the construction *have got* (I *have got* two goldfish), but never by itself (*I got* a cold). There is nothing grammatically wrong with using *got* in its proper form to mean *become*, *own*, or *acquire*. However, note that both usages are inappropriate for formal writing.

EXAMPLES: I *have gotten* better at throwing the Frisbee.

Selina's *got* her driver's license; let's have her drive today.

Where possible, avoid the word *got* in formal writing and substitute a more descriptive word. There is no reason to write "Mr. Ooze has got to realize that hat looks silly" when you could write "he must realize that his hat looks silly." Similarly, you do not need to write "it has gotten ten degrees colder" when you could write "the temperature has dropped ten degrees."

EXERCISE

In the following sentences, replace the underlined phrase with a more suitable, descriptive phrase.

It's got to be past eleven o'clock.

There is no reason to have gotten so upset at Wes.

150

Lester <u>has got</u> four younger sisters.
I <u>got</u> to <u>get</u> going.

87. Know the Difference Between the Verbs *Assure*, *Ensure*, and *Insure*

The similarity of spelling and pronunciation for these three words ensures the inevitable confusion of their usages. To *assure* is "to convince or guarantee a person"; to *ensure* is "to make an event certain"; and to *insure* is "to pay for financial loss."

EXAMPLES: I *assure* you that I will be on time for my appointment.

To *ensure* his comfort, Nick tucked an extra blanket into his bed.

Health coverage does not always *insure* the cost of dental check-ups.

Although it may seem simple to remember that *insure* refers to money (just think of insurance), it gets a bit more difficult keeping *assure* and *ensure* straight. *Assure* always refers to people, while *ensure* always refers to events.

EXERCISE

Choose the correct word in the following sentences:

Mr. Ooze (ensures/assures) me that his intentions are noble.

The passengers would like some (reassurance/reinsurance) that you know how to fly this plane.

Living in the flood zone, Mr. Ooze was forced to (ensure/insure) his house against natural disasters.

88. Know the Difference Between the Verbs *Accept* and *Except*

Accept means "to receive" or "to believe." *Except* means "to not include." Other than the similarity in pronunciation, there is no explanation for why these words are perennially confused with one another. Still, it is a very common mistake.

EXAMPLES: The Church now *accepts* divorce as a legitimate procedure.
I must *except* the broken dishes from being sold at the yard sale.

Except is more often used as a preposition than a verb. In these instances, be sure that it refers to the object of the sentence, not the subject.

EXAMPLE: Mr. Ooze likes all flavors *except* Purplesaurus Rex.

EXERCISE

Choose the correct words in the following sentences:

(Accept/Except) for the hurricane and the roaches, our vacation was a lot of fun.
Roger has been (accepted/excepted) at the university.
The speaker rudely (accepted/excepted) his supervisor when congratulating the company.

89. Know the Difference Between the Words *Affect* and *Effect*

Affect and *effect* are commonly confused because they look and sound like one another. Since both exist as nouns and verbs, it is important to learn the meanings for each before trying to guess which word to use.

Affect as a verb means "to influence how something occurs" or "to cultivate." *Affect* as a noun is obsolete except for its psychological context. (In other words, don't worry about its second definition.)

EXAMPLES: Will my topspin serve *affect* your ability to return the ball?

Although luxuriously wealthy, Mr. Ooze likes to *affect* a lifestyle of meager existence.

Effect as a verb means "to bring about." The most common usage of *effect* is as a noun, meaning "result."

EXAMPLES: The new Monopoly rules *effected* resentment and outrage from the children.

She never anticipated the *effect* that her book would have on readers.

A good way to remember that *effect* is most commonly used as a noun is to remember the two *e*'s in *the effect*.

EXERCISE

Choose the correct word in the following sentences:

Sherri (affected/effected) innocence when accused of stealing the last chocolate.
The dust inside his VCR (affects/effects) the quality of movies.
Snorting pepper (effects/affects) sneezing.

90. Know When to Use *As* and When to Use *Like* in Comparative Sentences

As is a conjunction and *like* is a preposition, but both are used to show a relationship or to make a comparison. *As* links verbs and verb phrases; *like* links nouns. This is the most important difference between them.

As means "serving the purpose of." Note in the following examples that verb phrases always follow the conjunction *as*.

EXAMPLES: He acts *as* a madman would act.
He acts *as* if he were surprised.

When coupled with *such* to form *such as*, it can be used to give examples. This construction is more similar to *like* in that *such as* acts like a preposition and is not followed by a verb phrase.

EXAMPLE: We bought items *such as* bread, milk, and butter.

Like means "similar to." It is used to form a simile, which means showing similarities between objects.

EXAMPLES: That cloud looks *like* a cow with wings.
It rained *like* the dickens that night.

Avoid informal constructions that use *like* as a conjunction, such as *you look like I feel*. It is grammatically proper to write *you look as I feel* because *as* must serve as a conjunction between the two verb phrases.

EXERCISE

Choose the best word or phrase in the following sentences:

Like a child, Mr. Ooze loves bright colors (as/such as/like) yellow, red, and blue.

It smells (like/as) burnt chicken in here.

You act (as if/like/as) our deal had never been made.

Some things, (as if/as/like) love, cannot be bought.

91. Know the Difference Between the Verbs *Can* and *May*

Can and *may* are often used interchangeably, but they do have different meanings. Both are "helping verbs," which means they assist in forming various tenses of another verb. *Can* refers to the ability to act; *may* refers to the potential to act.

EXAMPLES: Mr. Ooze *can* swim very well.
Mr. Ooze *may* swim tomorrow.
Mr. Ooze *can* swim, but he *may* decide not to.

Although common in informal speech, *can* should not be used to denote potential or permission. A child should ask if he *may* go out to play, not if he *can* go out to play.

EXERCISE

Choose the correct word in the following sentences:

Laurie (can/may) help the new secretary find the files.
You (can/may) be interested in hearing this news.
(Can/May) I show you to your table?

92. Know the Difference Between the Words *Complement* and *Compliment*

Similar spellings and almost identical pronunciations make these two words difficult to keep straight. *Complement* means "to make complete"; *compliment* means "to speak admiringly of." Both can be nouns or verbs.

EXAMPLES: The lemon sauce *complements* the fish perfectly.
The lemon sauce is a *complement* to the fish.
I should *compliment* Mr. Ooze on that lovely purple sweater.
Mr. Ooze deserves a *compliment* for his lovely purple sweater.

You can remember that *complement* means to *complete*. Note that the same root exists in both.

93. Avoid Fragments, Such as *Being the Leader* and *Have Gun, Will Hunt*

Fragments are incomplete pieces of sentences. They violate Rule 17, which states that every sentence requires a subject and a verb. Fragments can be words, phrases, or dependent clauses. For example:

WRONG: By mistake, Mr. Ooze stepped on Wes's tail. Instantly heard a loud cat yowl.

Here, "Instantly heard a loud cat yowl" is grammatically incorrect, because as a sentence, it lacks a subject. It would be better to write:

BETTER: By mistake, Mr. Ooze stepped on Wes's tail. He instantly heard a loud cat yowl.

or

BETTER: By mistake, Mr. Ooze stepped on Wes's tail, and he instantly heard a loud cat yowl.

In certain rare instances, fragments can be acceptable and even effective. Used deliberately and sparingly, they can be instrumental in catching the eye or adding emphasis. Only use them, however, in situations where you have some leeway as to style and correctness (in creative writing such as fiction or advertising, for example). Do not use them in an English paper; your teacher will almost certainly mark them as incorrect.

94. Avoid Run-On Sentences, Such as *I Am Good I Am Great*

Run-on sentences are not only grammatically incorrect, they are also extremely awkward. A run-on sentence starts out as a perfectly normal sentence, but it doesn't stop when it should. Like an unstoppable killer in a slasher movie, it just keeps going, piling on words and clauses.

BAD: There are two types of run-on sentences, the first kind is a comma splice.

The sentence above is a perfect example of a comma splice. In a comma splice, two independent clauses, or complete sentences, are separated only by a comma.

BAD: The second kind of run-on is a fused sentence in a fused sentence there is no comma.

Like a comma splice, a fused sentence incorrectly combines two independent clauses. In a fused sentence, however, the clauses are not separated by any kind of punctuation at all.

Correcting run-on sentences is usually very simple. Consider the following sentence and its various revisions:

BAD: Mr. Ooze was very happy he actually found himself enjoying being married.

- Use a period to create two sentences:

BETTER: Mr. Ooze was very happy. He actually found himself enjoying being married.

- Use a semicolon to offset both phrases:

BETTER: Mr. Ooze was very happy; he actually found himself enjoying being married.

- Use a coordinating conjunction to create one complex sentence:

BETTER: Mr. Ooze was very happy, *and* he actually found himself enjoying being married.

- Change the structure/wording to create one new sentence:

BETTER: Mr. Ooze was so happy that he found himself actually enjoying being married.

95. Avoid Dangling Modifiers, Such as *Mr. Mark Helps Us, the Friendly Neighbor*

When people want to show that something has gone drastically wrong in a piece of writing, they often point to dangling modifiers to prove their case. Any adjective, adverb, phrase, or clause modifies or describes something in a sentence. If it is not clear what the modifier refers to, or what its antecedent is, it is said to be dangling.

DANGLER: We saw the book in the window *walking back from the movie.*

In this example, it is unclear what is happening. As written, the sentence seems to imply that the book in the window was walking back from the movie, which obviously makes no sense. The italicized phrase, *walking back from the movie,* is meant to refer to the people who were doing the walking, but because the words are out of order, the meaning is lost.

CLEAR: Walking back from the movie, we saw the book in the window.

Now the meaning is revealed. *Walking back from the movie* is a participial phrase, which describes the people who saw the book.

The only way to avoid this problem is to check your work carefully. When you finish writing a draft, go back and reread it, and make sure that all of your modifiers are clearly connected to their referents.

EXERCISE

Connect or move the following modifiers so the sentences make sense.

Mr. Ooze was walking along when came at him a bird flying upside-down in a screaming dive.
He caught the bird and threw it into the pit yelling.
He began throwing dirt onto the bird and into the pit grabbing a shovel.
"Revenge is sweet, chicken-legs!" he cried laughing.

96. Don't Use Double Negatives, Such as *Isn't Nothing* or *Hasn't Not Gone*

Don't use double negatives: This is an old and famous grammatical rule which, for a change, makes sense. A double negative is created when you use two negative elements in a sentence. This occurs when people think that by using more words, it will add emphasis.

Unfortunately, standard English doesn't work that way with negatives. To say that "you *don't* know *nothing*" is self-contradictory; instead of intensifying the meaning, the two negatives cancel each other out. The speaker winds up saying the opposite of what was meant—"you do know something."

There are some words that have a negative element attached to them, as a prefix (for example, words like *unintentional* or *disagreeable*). When such words are combined with a negative adjective or adverb, the result is grammatically correct, but often stilted.

WEAK: He was *not disagreeable*; I just didn't like him.

BETTER: I didn't like him, even though he seemed agreeable enough.

166

The writer's meaning can be understood in the first example, but the reader has to work at it. The second example is clearer and more direct.

97. Don't Use Double Comparatives (Such as *More Friendlier*) or Superlatives (Such as *Most Friendliest*)

Sometimes people get carried away with adjectives. Trying to emphasize a point, they use so many adjectives that the reader feels as though he or she is being beaten around the head. This can get annoying, but it can get downright confusing with the comparative or superlative forms. Don't use double comparatives or superlatives; instead of intensifying your meaning, you will only obscure it.

Sometimes people use double forms because they forget which form of the comparative or superlative a word uses. So, they use both, just to be safe, but unfortunately that's a guaranteed mistake.

WRONG: Mr. Ooze said, "The pie you made tastes *more better* than Lisa's."

What happened here? Mr. Ooze is trying to say that the pie you baked tastes better than the one Lisa baked. Unfortunately, Mr. Ooze couldn't remember if the comparative form of *good* uses *more* as an auxiliary, as in "Dan is *more handsome* than Hal," or if it uses the word *better* (see Rules 25 and 26). Thus, Mr. Ooze the pie critic tried using both, and that's not right. The same thing would have happened if he had tried to say "Your pie tastes *more best*," instead of "Your pie tastes *best*."

Here's a hint. When you do need to use a helping

word like *more* or *less* to form a comparative or superlative form, you don't change the adjective itself
too. If you need to change the adjective itself in some
way, by adding *-er* or *-est* or something, you don't
need the helping word.

EXAMPLES: I am content . . . I am less content. (*Content* doesn't change, and a helping adjec-
tive was added.)

I am happy . . . I am happier. (*Happy*
changes, but there was no helping adjective added.)

98. Know That Words Like *Perfect* and *Ultimate* Should Not Be Used with Comparatives or Superlatives

Another common mistake that people make is to use comparative or superlative forms with words such as *perfect* or *ultimate*. If you think about it it's easy to see why this doesn't make sense.

If something is *perfect*, that means that there is absolutely nothing wrong with it, that every possible thing is as good as it can be. It cannot be improved. So how can anything be more than perfect, or "more perfect"?

By the same token, if something is the ultimate, that means it is the last. What does it mean to be the "most last"? This is meaningless. If you are standing in line, and you are last, you are at the end of the line; you are in the ultimate position. If I come and get in line after you, you are no longer in the ultimate position; I am.

If you're not sure if you should use a comparative or superlative form with the adjective you have in mind, think about the real meaning of the word. Then go look it up, to be sure.

99. Use Contractions, Such as *Can't* and *Aren't*, Correctly

In formal, written English, you probably won't use contractions very much, because they are generally considered too informal. However, when you do use them, make sure that you use them correctly. All too often, the casual habits of our spoken language carry over, and result in misspellings and confusion.

Some of the most common errors revolve around the proper spelling of contractions with the auxiliary verb *have*. This is correctly written as *'ve*, as in "I should've written this more clearly." Unfortunately, many people slur this phrase when they speak, and they then spell out the slurred form in their writing. The two most common errors are "I *should of* written . . ." and "I *shoulda* written. . . ."

Similar errors occur with prepositions. Instead of saying, "Get *out of* here," people yell, "Get *outta* here!" That's okay at the ballpark or in a fiction piece, but not when you're writing formal prose. Watch out for such carelessness in your own writing.

100. Differentiate Between *Its* and *It's*

The confusion between *its* and *it's* occurs so often that it deserves special mention.

Here is the answer.

CONTRACTION: *It's* is a contraction of the phrase *it is*.

POSSESSIVE: *Its* is the possessive form of the third-person singular pronoun *it*.

The confusion arises because people are logical, and (in this case, anyway) English is not. Most of the time, English uses the apostrophe + s form to indicate possession. So, people extend that rule to the pronoun *it*. Unfortunately, English uses the same form to contract the third person singular form of the verb *to be* (he is, she is, it is), and so a problem is born. The solution creates an exception (making the possessive form of the pronoun *its*) and many people forget this. However, the difference in meaning is real and important, so try to remember the distinction.

101. Watch Out for Sexist Language, Especially in Choosing Pronouns

Sexist language is now seen as offensive by many people. However it is not, strictly speaking, grammatically incorrect. The tragedy of modern English is that many people, trying to follow the laudable goal of fighting sexism, are creating some dreadful grammatical problems.

The most serious difficulties arise from the inconvenient fact that English has no gender-neutral, singular pronoun for people (*it* can only refer to animals or objects). Historically, the default has been to use the masculine form *he* when writing, with the disclaimer that it is understood to include *she* (the old phrase that students were told to remember was that "man embraces woman"). Now, however, this can (and often will) be interpreted as sexist.

You can frequently get around this problem by recasting your sentence in the plural; failing that, you may have to resort to the phrase *he or she*. Whatever you do, though, be consistent about it. Many problems occur when, in their haste to avoid sexism, people begin mixing plural pronouns with singular antecedents.

INCORRECT: *One member* of the crowd may interrupt the speech with *their* opinions.

TRADITIONAL: *One member* of the crowd may interrupt the speech with *his* opinions.

173

NONSEXIST: *One member* of the crowd may interrupt the speech with *his or her* opinions.

In the first example, the writer is either ignorant of, or is trying to avoid, stating whether or not the crowd member is male or female; but in either case a grammatical error is the result (the pronoun does not agree with its antecedent in number). In the traditional example, the writer has arbitrarily assigned a sex to the crowd member. It may or may not be correct; that could only be determined by context. In the nonsexist example, the writer has allowed for the possibility that the crowd member could be of either sex.

You should also be on the lookout for sexist words. Replace words such as *fireman* and *postman* with gender-neutral alternatives, such as *firefighter* and *postal worker*; this avoids the implicit suggestion that all firefighters or postal workers are men.

A note of warning on pronoun gender. Vehicles used for transportation, such as cars, boats, trains, or airplanes, have for many years been referred to as feminine (generally by their male pilots or drivers). For example, a race car driver may brag, "Out on the track, you'll see what *she* can do," referring to a favorite car. Such references have traditionally shown a casual form of affection, and many people still use them. However, some people now find this sort of terminology sexist and demeaning to women. In the end, *it* can always serve to identify an inanimate object.